T0191090

These Immortal Creations

These *Immortal Creations*

An Anthology of British Romantic Poetry

editedy by Sylvia Hunt

Universitas

Universitas Press

Montreal

U

www.universitaspress.com

First published in March 2017

Library and Archives Canada Cataloguing in Publication

These immortal creations : an anthology of British romantic poetry / edited by Sylvia Hunt.

ISBN 978-0-9950291-9-4 (softcover)

1. English poetry--19th century. I. Hunt, Sylvia, editor

PR1222.T44 2017   821'.7   C2017-901342-4

Printed by Ingram

Table of Contents

Introduction

Although only a very short period of time, the years between 1780 and 1830 were revolutionary ones, politically, socially and culturally. Now known as the Romantic Period and seen as the delineation between the Neoclassical and Victorian Periods, these fifty years saw rapid changes in the lives of almost all Britons. Politically, the enquiries into freedom, both personal and political, moved from theoretical discussion to tangible implementation. In the American colonies and in France, the philosophies of Kant, Rousseau and Locke framed the Declarations of Independence and Rights of Man. In England, social radicalism demanding political reform and universal suffrage was met with violence in the Peterloo Massacre, but would later result in reforms to suffrage and employment conditions. Women's demands for education and protections in marriage and under the law were seen by many to destabilize the patriarchal status quo, but would eventually lead to legislative changes. Slavery, an established part of colonial development, came to be seen as an abuse of the human rights so vehemently contested in Europe. Rapid advancements in science and technology changed all forms of life for everyone from factory workers to the wealthy: machines rapidly made ready-made goods; steam engines replaced animal and human labor; rapid transportation moved people and goods around the country and around the world; medicines prolonged life; and gas lighting illuminated the darkness. With the sudden overthrow of the French monarchy and the advance of a new social order, a fresh era heralded the end to oppressive aristocracies and the beginning of democratic ideals. Byron summarized this optimistic new age of transformation when he wrote:

> Talk not of seventy years as an age; in seven
> I have seen more changes, down from monarchs to
> The humblest individual under Heaven,
> Than might suffice a moderate century through.
> (*Don Juan* 11, ll. 649-652)

In this atmosphere of revolutionary energy, young writers could not help but be galvanized into creating new forms and experimenting with new ideas. We would come to call these writers the Romantics, a group of poets, novelists and polemicists who created works which were as aesthetically transformative as the times in which they lived.

The term *Romantic*, when used to describe the historical and cultural period of 1780-1830, is a product of the late nineteenth century and only came into widespread use in the early twentieth century as a defining label for specific writers.[1] Later, Romanticism became associated with certain political events (the French and American revolutions, the Napoleonic wars) and specific responses to those events.[2] For those living in the eighteenth century, *romantic* referred to the romances of the High Middle Ages and Renaissance (Sidney's *Arcadia* and Malory's *Morte d'Arthur*, for example); later, it became attached to a specific type of writing known as the prose romance and best exemplified in the novels of Matthew Lewis, Horace Walpole, Anne Radcliffe and Charlotte Dacre. In short, the term *romantic* identified any work that was considered fanciful, supernatural, or dealt with courtly love. These elements are also essential to the Romantic writers, but like any good artists, they transform the conventional aesthetic into something new. For example, the Romantics were less interested in exploring courtly, artificial love than they were in writing about a love of a greater scope: love of nature, love of freedom, love of humanity. The supernatural, so essential to medieval romances, became entwined with the Romantic aesthetic of the sublime (explained below). With respect to imagination, the old creative practices of the earlier literary periods accepted imitation as part of the creative process. For example, eighteenth-century critic Richard Hurd states that a striving for originality would only produce awkwardness, impropriety and affectation, and "all poets must be imitators since poetic merit lies only in execution and not in originality" (183). By the end of the century, however, the Romantics rejected imitation as legitimate creative expression, seeing it as derivative and antithetical to the notion of creation. William Blake wrote, "To Imitate I abhor," preferring "Art of Invention, not Imitation" (545). Wordsworth more fully outlined the Romantic manifesto in the preface to *The Lyrical Ballads* stating that

1 Hippolyte Taine was the first author to apply the terms "romantic" and "Romanticism" to these writers in his *History of English Literature* (1863).
2 William John Courthope in *The Romantic Movement in English Poetry: The Effects of the French Revolution* (1910) specifically connects the writers with liberal, radical, and revolutionary ideas.

he rejects the "common inheritance of Poets" (66) in preference for something new, natural and authentic.

Defining what is meant by *Romantic* has been a preoccupation for critics and scholars almost from the time that writers began producing poetry that was unlike Neoclassical literature. When modern readers study the poets considered to be part of the Romantic Movement, they often assume that the term *movement* connotes similar aesthetic ideals among its members. The term *member* itself implies a type of literary club with common interests or unifying philosophical ideals. However, we as readers need to realize that, while we now see common themes and aesthetic sensibilities, the poets did not see themselves as a movement. Any reading of their works clearly shows them to be different artistically, socially, and politically. In fact, they often saw difference instead of similarity and occasionally rejected the styles, politics, and beliefs of their contemporaries. The second generation of poets found fault with the first generation (Byron and Shelley, in particular, thought Wordsworth abandoned his political and creative ideals when he accepted the poet-laureateship); the range of social status pitted working-class poets (like Blake, Hunt, and Keats who were disparagingly labeled Cockneys) against the genteel or aristocratic poets (Wordsworth, Byron and Shelley); because of their gender, women were thought to be excluded from robust Romantic aesthetics; the religious devotion of Blake is contrasted with Shelley's equally devout atheism; poetic manifestos expressed different opinions about suitable content and form of expression. In general, however, there is an organic quality to the poetry produced by these writers in comparison to the mechanical nature of Neoclassicism. It is for this reason that we see them as a collective or movement that bridges the Neoclassical and the Victorian periods.

In order to understand Romanticism, it is necessary to understand the period in which the writers lived and the aesthetics and ideals which shaped their work.

THE PERIOD AND THE POETS

Despite the fact, as already stated, that the Romantics were varied in their poetic styles, there are some commonalities that connect them.

Philosophical Origins

Romantic creativeness finds its roots in late 17th-century philosophy. There are several philosophical branches that inspired this group of writers. The first deals with the creative or imaginative process; the second is political and inspired the writers personally and professionally.

For the writers of our period, reason, the revered attribute of humanity, is no longer thought to be the guiding principle of human life; instead it is individuality and the ability to give full expression to emotions, ideas and insights. With respect to the primacy of imagination, John Locke's *Essay Concerning Human Understanding* (1690) was an essential text. In that treatise, Locke argues against innate ideas and for the notion that the mind is a *tabula rasa*, or blank slate upon which impressions are laid. In addition, he argues that the mind is capable of creating images (the imagination) and gaining pleasure from those images. While Locke was primarily interested in how the mind worked, Anthony Ashley Cooper (1621-1683) was interested in the connection between morality and aesthetics. Throughout his *Characteristics of Men, Manners, Opinions, Times, etc.* (1711) he argues for the centrality of feeling in human life, stating that moral beauty is a "beauty of the sentiments, the grace of actions, the turn of characters, and the proportions of a human mind" (IV, 63). Human beings, he contends, have an instinctive goodness and an instinctive taste that will lead them to the virtuous and beautiful and away from the vicious and ugly. Cooper states that true self-knowledge comes from the study of the passions, claiming "This is because *I am* my passions: These passions, according as they have the ascendancy in me and differ in proportion with one another, affect my character and make me different with respect to myself and others" (III, 132).

Politically, Jean-Jacques Rousseau best captured the aspiration for freedom, both personal and political, with his statement "Man is born free, but everywhere he is in chains" (*The Social Contract*, 29). Man, he argues, is born good and noble when living in a state of nature. The development of civilizations and all that civilization entails, particularly the owning of property, corrupts natural man. This "right to the possessions of others" means that "equality was destroyed and followed by the most frightful disorder" (43). In his *Discourse on Inequality* (1754), he states, "Usurpations by the rich, robbery by the poor, and the unbridled passions of both, suppressed the cries of natural compassion and the still feeble voice of justice, and filled men with avarice, ambition and vice. Between the title of the strongest and that of the first occupier, there arose perpetual conflicts, which never ended but in battles and bloodshed" (29).

In England, Thomas Paine's *Rights of Man* (1791) attacked the monarchy and aristocracy (as institutions) as despotic organizations which deliberately suppress basic human rights. His demand for republicanism and social welfare was seen as seditious and a direct call to arms. Around the same time, William Godwin's influential polemic *Inquiry Concerning Political Justice* (1793) would argue many of the same points as Rousseau and Paine: that all men are equal; institutions like the church, the government, the social ranking of people, and marriage are all designed to hold men in check. Godwin saw Man as inherently perfectible, but, unlike Paine, his vision of change was gradual and non-violent.

All of these philosophical works had an influence on contemporary political and creative thought. Social and political reform was hotly debated in salons and newspapers, so-much-so that the government passed the Treason Act and Seditious Meetings Act in 1795, making it difficult, if not illegal, to discuss reform. James Leigh Hunt would spend two years in prison on the charge of sedition for an article he published in his newspaper *The Examiner* attacking the Prince Regent. Regular visitors to his cell included George Gordon, Charles Lamb, and radical parliamentarian Henry Brougham. Percy Shelley, close friend with Hunt, was an acolyte of Godwin, introducing himself to the philosopher and, in the process, meeting his daughter Mary. Many of the poems included in this anthology deal with the political events, debates, and philosophies of the period.

Political upheaval

From the Enlightenment's philosophical ideas developed the great political movements of the period. In 1775, the American colonies revolted against what they saw to be the tyrannical rule of George III. In 1789, Paris mobs stormed the Bastille chanting "Liberté, Equalité, Fraternité." Within a few short months, the Bourbon monarchy was toppled and, for a short time, it appeared that the promise of a utopian democracy was finally within reach. As Wordsworth wrote, "the whole

Earth,/ The beauty wore of promise" ("French Revolution", ll 13-14). It was this utopian dream that inspired young Coleridge and Southey to plan their own ideal community, Pantisocracy, in the new American republic. It was the optimism of Godwin's political treatise that galvanized young, idealistic people like Percy Shelley, who, tired of class prejudice and monarchies, agitated for change that would improve the lives of all Britons. Unfortunately, this utopian promise quickly slid into the horrors of the Reign of Terror, followed by Napoleon's coup in 1799, European war, and, in the end, the restoration of the Bourbon monarchy. The Romantics of both generations despaired as the republican dream was replaced with despotic reality.

In England, initial reaction to the French Revolution was generally positive; it was seen as the French finally throwing off their antiquated, oppressive feudal system for a more democratic government. In November 1789, Richard Price (1723-1791) sermonized

> "Liberty is the next great blessing which I have mentioned as the object of patriotic zeal. It is inseparable from knowledge and virtue and together with them completes the glory of a community. An enlightened and virtuous country must be a free country. . . . Behold, the light you [defenders of freedom] have struck out, after setting America free, reflected to France and there kindled into a blaze that lays despotism in ashes and warms and illuminates Europe!" (*Discourse*).

Price's comments spurred Edmund Burke to write *Reflections on the Revolution in France* (1791), a conservative, alarmist view of the revolution. Burke prophesied that the revolution would mean the destruction of France and lead to European war. What followed was a war of pamphlets, escalating into political rhetoric with reformers metaphorically tarred with all the excesses of the revolution. The reformers retaliated with novels, songs, poetry and caricature, and probably the most potent pamphlet on governmental reform and freedom: Thomas Paine's *Rights of Man* (1792). The English government responded in 1792 with a Royal Proclamation Against Seditious Writing; anything perceived to be revolutionary, including discussions about ending the slave trade and the rights of women, was dangerous and in need of suppression. Thus, England, initially seen as a model of democracy in Europe (when compared with the antiquated French regime) became as despotic as France.

Wordsworth, Coleridge, and Southey initially sympathized with the principles of the Revolution. Wordsworth translated Man's equality into his use of the "very language of men" and using what would normally be seen as "unworthy" subject matter (Preface, *Lyrical Ballads*, 65, 84), namely rural workers, peasant classes, and rustic landscapes. This political enthusiasm waned with the execution of Louis XVI and the Reign of Terror. The second generation of poets, particularly Byron and Shelley, maintained their idealism, viewing Napoleon as the hero of liberty and democracy until he regressed into a dictator himself.

Not all Romantic poets supported the French Revolution. Hannah More, for example, was a radical who agitated for emancipation of slaves and for female educational reform. However, she was vocal in her rejection republican ideals, and her *Cheap Repository Tracts* were written specifically for distribution among the poor in an attempt to diffuse revolutionary ideas.

The Aesthetic of the Sublime and the Beautiful

The prime aesthetic of the Romantic writers is known as the sublime with its antithesis as the beautiful. To define the two terms *the sublime* and *the beautiful* is as difficult as it is to define Romantic. Numerous authors in the late eighteenth century attempted such a definition, Immanuel Kant (1724-1804) and Edmund Burke (1729-1797) being the most famous. In general, these two terms represent the end points on a spectrum of reaction to an event, an object, or a landscape. The sublime, according to Kant, is associated with, "what is absolutely great," producing an "agitation of the mind" (107) which must then be processed or the beholder of the sublime will live in a constant state of terror. For Kant, then, reason is an essential component of the aesthetic experience; reason processes the imaginative response to an object or event. Thus, from emotion/imagination comes an enlarged understanding due to the reasoning process. In similar fashion, Burke's *A Philosophical Enquiry into the Origins of the Our Ideas of the Sublime and Beautiful* (1757) equates the sublime with notions of danger, terror and the terrible, all of which are "productive of the strongest emotion which the mind is capable of feeling" (45). Mountain ranges, storms, darkness, obscurity, power, "Whatever is fitted," according to Burke, "in any sort to excite the ideas of pain, and danger, that is to say, whatever is in any sort terrible, or is conversant about terrible objects, or operates in a manner analogous to terror, is a source of the sublime" (74). For Burke, terror elicits a sense of pleasure; the observer of the sublime is thrilled with the experience of terror. For that reason, distance or an element of safety is necessary to ensure delight. Unlike Kant, Burke finds the imagination and the imaginative response to be more powerful in the sublime experience.

Beauty, according to Burke, is the antithesis of the sublime. It is associated with smallness, smoothness, and weakness. In many ways, this aesthetic system is gendered, with sublimity associated with the masculine (power, size, danger) and beauty with the feminine (weakness, diminutiveness, safety). If the sublime provokes terror, beauty's response is simply pleasure. As material for the artist, the sublime was often seen as inappropriate for or incomprehensible to female artists. As this anthology will show, however, women did participate in articulating sublimity. In fact, they demonstrate that the female experience (childbirth, motherhood) is itself sublime.

Our poets deal almost exclusively with the sublime: events (the Ancient Mariner's ghost ship, Prometheus' defiant act and his eternal punishment, European war, revolution), landscapes (mountains, vibrant daffodils, woodlands), and characters (madmen, revolutionaries). In "Hymn to Intellectual Beauty," Shelley describes a personal epiphany as a physical encounter with the Spirit of Beauty: "Sudden thy shadow fell on me;/ I shrieked and clasped my hands in ecstacy!" (ll. 59-60). Both terrific and sensual, this encounter transforms Shelley, spiritually and creatively. Wordsworth attempts to describe his own encounter with the sublime when he writes:

> ...it appeared to me
> The perfect image of a might Mind,
> Of one that feeds upon infinity,
> That is exalted by an underpresence,
> The sense of God, or whatso'er is dim
> Or vast in its own being
> With circumstance most awful and sublime
> (*Prelude*, XIII, ll. 70-76)

The sublime transformed with poet personally and creatively. Their poems attempt to transfer this experience to the reader in an attempt to elicit similar revolution on a personal, spiritual, creative level.

IDEALS OF ROMANTIC POETRY

The Poet

The Romantic poet is both man and myth.[3] He inherits an ancient birthright and creates a new heritage. He is prophet, seer, priest, bard, creator of (imaginative) worlds, hero, and myth-maker. He is also a man speaking to other men. Wordsworth described his poetic 'calling' when he wrote "poetic numbers came/ Spontaneously, and cloth'd in priestly robe/ My spirit, thus singled out, as it might seem,/ For holy services" (*Prelude* 1.ll 61-64). Blake demanded that his readers "Hear the voice of the Bard" ("Introduction," *Songs of Experience*). Coleridge states that the poet is a powerful figure who "brings the whole soul of man into activity" (*Biographia Literaria*, chap. 14). He ends "Kubla Khan" with a vision of the poet as an otherworldly being who must be confined in a holy circle. Byron produced poems filled with Byronic heroes who, like their creator, are outcasts, alienated from the human race by sensibilities too acute for normal men. The poet may share a common humanity, but he is endowed with "more lively sensibility, more enthusiasm and tenderness, who has a greater knowledge of human nature, and a more comprehensive soul" than his fellow men (Wordsworth, Preface, *Lyrical Ballads*, 71). Poets are, according to Shelley, the vehicles for the spirit of the age and for the ages to come; they are "the unacknowledged legislators of the world" (Shelley 118). In fact, in his *Defense of Poetry* (1821), Shelley endows both poetry and the poet with divine power, labeling the former "immortal creations" (77) and the latter a person who "participates in the eternal, the infinite and the one" (79).

Imagination as truth and the subjective experience

The poets in this anthology would all define imagination differently; however, they all have espoused the primacy of imagination and placed it as the root source for creativity. The mind was seen as having a visionary power in its creative capabilities. Imagination is not simply the ability to craft mental pictures; the creative powers of the mind also generate truths. As Byron states in *Childe Harold's Pilgrimage*, "The

3 It is against this glorified male image that female poets had to compete.

beings of the mind are not of clay;/ Essentially immortal, they create/ And multiply in us a brighter ray/And more beloved existence/ . . ./ Watering the heart whose early flowers have died,/And with a fresher growth replenishing the void" (Canto IV, ll. 37-45). Imagination is, according to Coleridge, "the living Power and prime Agent of all human perception" (*Biographia Literaria* Chap. 13). Blake declared that imagination can "see a World in a Grain of Sand/And a Heaven in a Wild Flower" ("Auguries of Innocence", ll. 1-2). Wordsworth wrote that "Imagination . . . in truth/ Is but another name for absolute power/ And clearest insight" (*Prelude* 14, ll. 190-192).

In addition to being endowed with acute insights or truths, the Romantic poet is no longer the urban, urbane 'rambler,' 'spectator' or 'observer' of the Neoclassical period whose observations are impartial and impersonal. Eighteenth-century Enlightenment philosophy upheld objective, verifiable truth and viewed the world as measurable, concrete, and with a common base of experience. The poets in this anthology present observations that are entirely subjective and deeply personal. These personal reflections, however, are meant to find community or commonality with readers. In a mechanized age which saw the breakdown of old, tight-knit social networks, the Romantics viewed their work as a means by which communities can be built around literatures of shared experience.

Language and form

In order to create these communities with readers, poetic tradition had to be reinvented, rejected, or modified. The cultured, convoluted, metaphoric language used by previous poets was replaced with simpler, more natural language. In short, poetry must not be labored. Instead, it should rise out of "the spontaneous overflow of powerful feelings . . . recollected in tranquility" (Wordsworth, Preface, *Lyrical Ballads*, 82).

With respect to form for Neoclassical poets like Dryden and Pope, the heroic couplet was the polished medium of expression, and form was ruled by classical ideals or "RULES of old discovered, not devised" (Pope, *An Essay on Criticism* 88). Wordsworth emphasized the importance of language in poetry so that clear ideas or passions can be conveyed to the reader. In particular, he felt it was essential to avoid "the phrases and figures of speech which from father to son have long been regarded as the common inheritance of Poets" (Preface, *Lyrical Ballads* 66). Language was no longer to be the sophisticated diction of the Neoclassicals, but the "language really spoken by men" (69). Coleridge would come to disagree with many of Wordsworth's statements about poetry as it related to their collaboration in the *Lyrical Ballads*. However, despite his fascination with the fantastical, his own poetry is preoccupied with the natural and simple, in the use of the vernacular, and the perfection of the rhythms of conversation in poems like "Frost at Midnight" and "This Lime-tree Bower My Prison."

The Romantics were not only adventurous and even playful experimenters with meter and rhyme. They also re-introduced older poetic forms like the ballad and sonnet. Ballads (traditionally associated with folk culture) were used by Wordsworth, Blake, Coleridge and Scott. Interested in the language and lifestyles of common men, it is natural that these poets would use a poetic form (the narrative song) associated with the working classes. For the second generation of poets, particularly Shelley and Keats, the sonnet was the favored form. These two artists in particular used it as the medium to explore the serious topics of politics, art, and mortality. Charlotte Smith, an early Romantic, used the sonnet form in order to have her work taken seriously since the form itself denoted high art.

The use of vernacular did not just pertain to the English poets, but also to the Scottish poets who used their dialect for artistic and political purposes. With the unification of Scotland and England in 1706, a union to which most of the population in Scotland objected, Scottish poets used language as a way to articulate cultural difference. To read Burns is to read culture; it requires that the reader assume the Scottish brogue. To read Scott requires that the reader have knowledge of Scottish history, a history rife with English conflict. By using dialect, the language of the 'common' Scotsman, and by using history (or mythology) as subject matter, the Scottish Romantics were performing their own type of revolution, a cultural one, in the confines of their new union with England.

Nature

The Romantic poets were diverse in their subject interests; Wordsworth's incidents from common life could not be more different from Coleridge's fantastical landscapes and characters; Byron's brooding, self-absorbed, misanthropic heroes contrast with

Keats's personal expressions of artistic inadequacy; Shelley's political pessimism contrasts with Leigh Hunt's social optimism; Blake's religious mysticism is antithetical to Shelley's atheism. However, one connecting theme which runs through their works is that of nature. These writers inherited a Newtonian image of nature, one that is rational, scientific, understood and understandable. Our Romantics found this vision too limiting, too static. The sublime aesthetic reanimated the natural universe with energy and vitality—nature was organic and dynamic. It was also concrete, real, changeable and a life-giving force. Each poet encounters the natural world in a different way. For Wordsworth, it is the simplicity of Nature that nourishes his natural man in his rustic condition. Coleridge finds manifest, gothic power in Nature. For Shelley and Keats, it is the moving clouds, skylarks and winds that inspire poets. Smith's brooding melancholy is mirrored in the natural world around her. Even Byron's Childe Harold, ostracized from civilized society, finds refuge and solace in the remote outposts of Europe.

Female Romantics

Up until the 1980s, the Romantic Movement was associated with men's writing. The 'big six' of Wordsworth, Coleridge, Blake, Shelley, Byron and Keats dominated most syllabi in university literature courses. In the eighteenth and early nineteenth centuries, the publication industry was male and not always receptive to women authors. English culture, in general, viewed female publication (or female authority for that matter) as transgressive. Women had long faced opposition, if not virulent animosity, if they dared enter into any arena deemed masculine. In particular any woman who even approached intellectualism was deemed a blue stocking and under suspicion of being "unsex'd" (Polwhele, "The Unsex'd Females"). The journal *British Critic* soundly denounced such women as antithetical to proper British society: "We heartily abjure Blue Stockings. We make no compromise with any variation of colour, from sky-blue to Prussian blue, blue stockings are an outrage upon the eternal fitness of things. It is a principle with us to regard an Academicienne of this Society, with the same charity that a cat regards a vagabond mouse" (quoted in Newlyn, 228). In light of comments like this one, it is not surprising that any woman who did dare become an author only produced things deemed appropriate for the sex: children's books, conduct literature, cook books, novels of manners and sentimental poems.

Despite this animosity, about a quarter of those considered to be members of the Romantic canon are actually women. Writers like More, Barbauld, Robinson, Smith and Hemans earned both reputation and a living by writing. In fact, Felicia Hemans was the most admired poet in her day. However, these women generally avoided political commentary since it was male-privileged territory; instead, authors like Barbauld look at female life and find it sublime; washing day is a Herculean event; pregnancy and birth are the definition of Nature and natural. More, who advocated for female education and the emancipation of slaves, participated in political discussion only as a conservative upholding traditional British values. Smith's elegiac sonnets influenced writers like Wordsworth and Coleridge and reflect the horrors of patriarchal restrictions on women.

For women, publication was seen as a form of prostitution or self-exposure. As Michael Baron states, "publication is like marriage; a woman loses her name" (178). Despite these dangers (or perhaps because of them), the female poets of the Romantic Movement found self-empowerment in the construction, articulation and publication of a feminized poetic identity.

THIS ANTHOLOGY

In *Reading Pictures*, Alberto Manguel pointed out the prime fault of books which look at a specific artist's output: "the fat volumes of a writer's collected works . . . seem to ignore the piecemeal cadence of an artist's offerings, suggesting instead one single and colossal output, instantaneous, uninterrupted and all-encompassing" (23). Instead, he claims, a work of art needs to be placed "among works of art created before and after it" so that we, the readers, can hear "the dialogue a painting or sculpture [or poem] established with other paintings or sculptures [or poems]" (13). This volume attempts to do the same thing; poems are placed with poems written around the same time by other authors. Instead of the standard anthological organization of grouping poems written by each author, the organization of this anthology is chronological; readers will be able to see poetic developments over the era known as the Romantic Period.

The selection process for the poems and authors was based on several factors. First, syllabi of Romantic literature courses were studied and the works most commonly appearing were considered for inclusion. Shorter works were, in general, preferred over longer ones; for example, Wordsworth's *Prelude* and Byron's *Don Juan* were excluded largely due to their length. Students are often deterred from reading poetic works of considerable length. Instead, shorter poems were selected. Some exceptions had to be made to this rule: Coleridge's *Ryme of the Ancyent Marinere* is an essential poem to the understanding of Coleridge and to early Romanticism. In this case, the original 1798 version was selected instead of the revised version that appeared in the 1800 edition of the *Lyrical Ballads*. With some exceptions, when it can be shown that the authors themselves have made minor changes, the texts have been preserved in the form given when first published. The poems are presented here in the chronological order of the year when they were written, even if they were sometimes published years or even decades later. Some poems are included that have rarely been anthologized before (Rogers, Williams, Landon, Hunt for example). These poets were popular and influential in their time and, thus, are essential in the study of the Romantic movement.

Various themes are suggested for the study of these works. These include:

- The poet as sage, prophet, minstrel, bard.
- Form—the unstructured form and lack of rhyme used by the early poets compared to the use of sonnet form and rhyming couplet of later ones; the use of songs and ballads.
- Politics, revolution, slavery.
- Nature as inspiration and ultimate form of art
- The various 'schools' of Romantic poets (Lake, Cockney, Satanic)
- The use of other poets' works as inspiration, or responding to other poets in the form of a poem
- Common subject matter (skylarks and nightingales; children; shipwrecks, etc.)
- First generation poets compared to the second generation
- How the artists respond to art and the creation of art
- Female poetic engagement with the sublime
- The supernatural or gothic
- Language (the elevated style of the sonnet; the dialect used by Scottish poets; the Wordworthian language of the common man).

Works Cited

Baron, Michael. *Language and Relationship in Wordsworth's Writing.* London: Longman, 1995.

Blake, William. *The Portable Blake.* Ed. Alfred Kazin. New York: Viking, 1955.

Burke, Edmund, *A Philosophical Enquiry into the Origin of our Ideas of the Sublime and Beautiful,* Ed. Adam Phillips. London: Oxford UP, 1990.

Byron, George Gordon. "Don Juan." *The Complete Poetical Works.* Ed. Jerome McGann. Vol. V. London, Oxford U.P., 1986.

Coleridge, Samuel Taylor. *Biographia Literaria.* Ed. James Engell and Walter Jackson Bate. Princeton, Princeton UP, 1983.

Hurd, Richard. "A Discourse Concerning Poetic Imitation." In *Q. Horatii Flacci: Epistola ad Augustum with an English Commentary and Notes to which is added A Discourse Concerning Poetic Imitation,* 109-241. London: Thurlbourn, 1753.

Kant, Immanuel. *Critique of Judgment.* Translated by Werner S. Pluhar. Indianapolis, Hackett Publishing Co., 1987.

Manguel, Alberto. *Reading Pictures: What we think about when we look at art.* New York: Random House, 2000.

Polwhele, Richard. "The Unsex'd Females." *Longman Anthology of British Literature: The Romantics.* Ed. Susan Wolfson and Peter Manning. New York: Longman: 2006.

Price, Richard. *A Discourse on the Love of our Country, delivered on Nov. 4, 1789, at the Meeting-House in the Old Jewry, to the Society for Commemorating the Revolution in Great Britain.* http://www.constitution.org/price/price_8.htm.

Rousseau, Jean-Jacques. *Du Contrat Social.* Paris: GF, 1992.

————. "Discourse on Inequality." *Rousseau's Political Writings.* Trans. G.D.H. Cole. New York: W.W. Norton, 1988.

Shaftesbury, Anthony Ashley Cooper, Third Earl of. *Characteristics of Men, Manners, Opinions, Times.* Ed. Lawrence E. Klein. Cambridge: Cambridge U.P., 1999.

Shelley, Percy. "A Defense of Poetry." *Selected Prose Works of Shelley.* Ed. Henry S. Salt London: Watts & Co., 1915 (75-118).

Wordsworth, William. *The Prelude, or Growth of a Poet's Mind.* Ed. Ernest de Selincourt. London: Oxford U.P., 1969.

1786

IN THE CHARACTER OF A RUINED FARMER
Robert Burns

The sun he is sunk in the west,
All creatures retired to rest,
While here I sit, all sore beset,
With sorrow, grief, and woe:
And it's O, fickle Fortune, O!

The prosperous man is asleep,
Nor hears how the whirlwinds sweep;
But Misery and I must watch
The surly tempest blow:
And it's O, fickle Fortune, O!

There lies the dear Partner of my breast;
Her cares for a moment at rest:
Must I see thee, my youthful pride,
Thus brought so very low!
And it's O, fickle Fortune, O!

There lie my sweet babies in her arms;
No anxious fear their little hearts alarms;
But for their sake my heart does ache,
With many a bitter throe:
And it's O, fickle Fortune, O!

1786

I once was by Fortune carest:
I once could relieve the distrest:
Now life's poor support, hardly earn'd
My fate will scarce bestow:
And it's O, fickle Fortune, O!

No comfort, no comfort I have!
How welcome to me were the grave!
But then my wife and children dear
O, wither would they go!
And it's O, fickle Fortune, O!

O whither, O whither shall I turn!
All friendless, forsaken, forlorn!
For, in this world, Rest or Peace
I never more shall know!
And it's O, fickle Fortune, O!

TO A MOUSE ON TURNING HER UP IN HER NEST WITH THE PLOUGH

Robert Burns

Wee, sleeket, cowran, tim'rous beastie,
O, what a panic's in thy breastie!
Thou need na start awa sae hasty,
      Wi' bickerin' brattle!
I wad be laith to rin an' chase thee
      Wi' murd'ring pattle!

I'm truly sorry Man's dominion
Has broken Nature's social union,
An' justifies that ill opinion,
      Which makes thee startle,
At me, thy poor, earth-born companion,
      An' fellow-mortal!

1786

I doubt na, whyles, but thou may thieve;
What then? poor beastie, thou maun live!
A daimen-icker in a thrave
      'S a sma' request:
I'll get a blessin wi' the lave,
      An' never miss't!

Thy wee-bit housie, too, in ruin!
It's silly wa's the win's are strewin!
An' naething, now, to big a new ane,
      O' foggage green!
An' bleak December's winds ensuin,
      Baithsnell an' keen!

Thou saw the fields laid bare an' waste,
An' weary Winter comin fast,
An' cozie here, beneath the blast,
      Thou thought to dwell,
Till crash! the cruel coulter past
      Out thro' thy cell.

That wee-bit heap o' leaves an' stibble
Has cost thee monie a weary nibble!
Now thou's turn'd out, for a' thy trouble,
      But house or hald,
To thole the Winter's sleety dribble,
      An' cranreuch cauld!

But Mousie, thou art no thy lane,
In proving foresight may be vain:
The best laid schemes o' mice an' men
      Gang aft agley,
An' lea'e us nought but grief an' pain,
      For promis'd joy!

Still, thou art blest, compar'd wi' me!
The present only toucheth thee:
But Och! I backward cast my e'e,
      On prospects drear!
An' forward tho' I canna see,
      I guess an' fear!

1786

1788

THE NEGRO'S COMPLAINT

William Cowper

Forc'd from home and all its pleasures,
    Afric's coast I left forlorn;
To increase a stranger's treasures,
    O'er the raging billows borne.

Men from England bought and sold me,
    Paid my price in paltry gold;
But, though slave they have enroll'd me,
    Minds are never to be sold.

Still in thought as free as ever,
    What are England's rights, I ask,
Me from my delights to sever,
    Me to torture, me to task?

Fleecy locks and black complexion
    Cannot forfeit Nature's claim;
Skins may differ, but affection
    Dwells in white and black the same.

Why did all-creating Nature
    Make the plant for which we toil?
Sighs must fan it, tears must water,
    Sweat of ours must dress the soil.

Think, ye masters iron-hearted,
    Lolling at your jovial boards,
Think how many backs have smarted
    For the sweets your cane affords.

Is there, as ye sometimes tell us,
    Is there One who reigns on high?
Has He bid you buy and sell us,
    Speaking from his throne, the sky?

Ask Him, if your knotted scourges,
    Matches, blood-extorting screws,
Are the means that duty urges
    Agents of his will to use?

Hark! He answers!—Wild tornadoes
    Strewing yonder sea with wrecks,
Wasting towns, plantations, meadows,
    Are the voice with which He speaks.

He, foreseeing what vexations
    Afric's sons should undergo,
Fixed their tyrants' habitations
    Where his whirlwinds answer—"No."

By our blood in Afric wasted
    Ere our necks received the chain;
By the miseries that we tasted,
    Crossing in your barks the main;

By our sufferings, since ye brought us
    To the man-degrading mart,
All sustained by patience, taught us
    Only by a broken heart;

Deem our nation brutes no longer,
    Till some reason ye shall find
Worthier of regard and stronger
    Than the colour of our kind.

Slaves of gold, whose sordid dealings
    Tarnish all your boasted powers,
Prove that you have human feelings,
    Ere you proudly question ours!

1788

1789

SONNET WRITTEN IN THE CHURCH YARD
AT MIDDLETON IN SUSSEX
Charlotte Smith

Press'd by the Moon, mute arbitress of tides,
   While the loud equinox its power combines,
   The sea no more its swelling surge confines,
But o'er the shrinking land sublimely rides.
The wild blast, rising from the Western cave,
   Drives the huge billows from their heaving bed;
   Tears from their grassy tombs the village dead,
And breaks the silent sabbath of the grave!
With shells and sea-weed mingled, on the shore
   Lo! their bones whiten in the frequent wave;
   But vain to them the winds and waters rave;
They hear the warring elements no more:
While I am doom'd—by life's long storm opprest,
To gaze with envy, on their gloomy rest.

1789

SONNET XXVII: SIGHING I SEE YON LITTLE TROOP
Charlotte Smith

Sighing I see yon little troop at play,
   By sorrow yet untouch'd; unhurt by care;
While free and sportive they enjoy to-day,
   "Content and careless of to-morrow's fare!"[1]
O happy age! when Hope's unclouded ray
   Lights their green path, and prompts their simple mirth,
E'er yet they feel the thorns that lurking lay
   To wound the wretched pilgrims of the earth,
Making them rue the hour that gave them birth,
   And threw them on a world so full of pain,
Where prosperous folly treads on patient worth,
   And, to deaf pride, misfortune pleads in vain!
Ah!—for their future fate how many fears
Oppress my heart—and fill mine eyes with tears!

---

1 The line, as Smith indicates in a note, is quoted from James Thomson.

SONNET: TO THE POPPY

Anna Seward

While Summer Roses all their glory yield
  To crown the Votary of Love and Joy,
  Misfortune's Victim hails, with many a sigh,
  Thee, scarlet POPPY of the pathless field,
Gaudy, yet wild and lone; no leaf to shield
  Thy flaccid vest, that, as the gale blows high,
  Flaps, and alternate folds around thy head.—
  So stands in the long grass a love-craz'd Maid,
Smiling aghast; while stream to every wind
  Her garish ribbons, smear'd with dust and rain;
  But brain-sick visions cheat her tortur'd mind,
And bring false peace. Thus, lulling grief and pain,
  Kind dreams oblivious from thy juice proceed,
  THOU FLIMSY, SHEWY, MELANCHOLY WEED.

From SONGS OF INNOCENCE   1789

William Blake

INTRODUCTION

Piping down the valleys wild
Piping songs of pleasant glee
On a cloud I saw a child.
And he laughing said to me.

Pipe a song about a Lamb;
So I piped with merry chear,
Piper pipe that song again—
So I piped, he wept to hear.

Drop thy pipe thy happy pipe
Sing thy songs of happy chear.
So I sung the same again
While he wept with joy to hear

Piper sit thee down and write
In a book that all may read—
So he vanish'd from my sight.
And I pluck'd a hollow reed.

And I made a rural pen,
And I stain'd the water clear,
And I wrote my happy songs
Every child may joy to hear

THE LITTLE BLACK BOY

William Blake

My mother bore me in the southern wild,
And I am black, but O! my soul is white;
White as an angel is the English child:
But I am black as if bereav'd of light.

1789

My mother taught me underneath a tree
And sitting down before the heat of day,
She took me on her lap and kissed me,
And pointing to the east began to say.

Look on the rising sun: there God does live
And gives his light, and gives his heat away.
And flowers and trees and beasts and men recieve
Comfort in morning joy in the noonday.

And we are put on earth a little space,
That we may learn to bear the beams of love,
And these black bodies and this sun-burnt face
Is but a cloud, and like a shady grove.

For when our souls have learn'd the heat to bear
The cloud will vanish we shall hear his voice.
Saying: come out from the grove my love & care,
And round my golden tent like lambs rejoice.

Thus did my mother say and kissed me,
And thus I say to little English boy.
When I from black and he from white cloud free,
And round the tent of God like lambs we joy:

Ill shade him from the heat till he can bear,
To lean in joy upon our fathers knee.
And then I'll stand and stroke his silver hair,
And be like him and he will then love me.

THE CHIMNEY SWEEPER

William Blake

When my mother died I was very young,
And my father sold me while yet my tongue
Could scarcely cry weep weep weep weep.
So your chimneys I sweep & in soot I sleep.

Theres little Tom Dacre, who cried when his head
That curled like a lambs back, was shav'd, so I said,
Hush, Tom never mind it, for when your head's bare,
You know that the soot cannot spoil your white hair.

1789

And so he was quiet, & that very night,
As Tom was a-sleeping he had such a sight,
That thousands of sweepers Dick, Joe Ned, & Jack,
Were all of them lock'd up in coffins of black

And by came an Angel who had a bright key,
And he open'd the coffins & set them all free;
Then down a green plain leaping laughing they run
And wash in a river and shine in the Sun.

Then naked & white, all their bags left behind,
They rise upon clouds, and sport in the wind.
And the Angel told Tom if he'd be a good boy,
He'd have God for his father & never want joy.

And so Tom awoke and we rose in the dark
And got with our bags & our brushes to work.
Tho' the morning was cold, Tom was happy & warm,
So if all do their duty, they need not fear harm.

THE LITTLE BOY LOST

William Blake

Father, father, where are you going
O do not walk so fast.
Speak father, speak to your little boy
Or else I shall be lost,

The night was dark no father was there
The child was wet with dew.
The mire was deep, & the child did weep
 And away the vapour flew.

THE LITTLE BOY FOUND

William Blake

1789

The little boy lost in the lonely fen,
Led by the wand'ring light,
Began to cry; but God ever nigh,
Appeared like his father in white.

He kissed the child & by the hand led
And to his mother brought,
Who in sorrow pale, thro' the lonely dale
Her little boy weeping sought.

HOLY THURSDAY

William Blake

Twas on a Holy Thursday their innocent faces clean
The children walking two & two in red & blue & green
Grey-headed beadles walkd before with wands as white as snow,
Till into the high dome of Pauls they like Thames waters flow

O what a multitude they seemd these flowers of London town
Seated in companies they sit with radiance all their own
The hum of multitudes was there but multitudes of lambs
Thousands of little boys & girls raising their innocent hands

Now like a mighty wind they raise to heaven the voice of song
Or like harmonious thunderings the seats of Heaven among
Beneath them sit the aged men wise guardians of the poor
Then cherish pity, lest you drive an angel from your door

THE LAMB

William Blake

Little Lamb who made thee
Dost thou know who made thee
Gave thee life & bid thee feed.
By the stream & o'er the mead;
Gave thee clothing of delight,
Softest clothing wooly bright;
Gave thee such a tender voice,
Making all the vales rejoice:
    Little Lamb who made thee
    Dost thou know who made thee

    Little Lamb I'll tell thee,
    Little Lamb I'll tell thee
He is called by thy name,
For he calls himself a Lamb:
He is meek & he is mild,
He became a little child:
I a child & thou a lamb,
We are called by his name.
    Little Lamb God bless thee
    Little Lamb God bless thee

1789

1790

THUNDER

Joanna Baillie

Spirit of strength, to whom in wrath 'tis given
To mar the earth, and shake the vasty heaven:
Behold the gloomy robes, that spreading hide
Thy secret majesty, lo! slow and wide,
Thy heavy skirts sail in the middle air,
Thy sultry shroud is o'er the noonday glare:
Th' advancing clouds sublimely roll'd on high,
Deep in their pitchy volumes clothe the sky:
Like hosts of gath'ring foes array'd in death,
Dread hangs their gloom upon the earth beneath.
It is thy hour: the awful deep is still,
And laid to rest the wind of ev'ry hill.
Wild creatures of the forest homeward scour,
And in their dens with fear unwonted cow'r.
Pride in the lordly palace is forgot;
And in the lowly shelter of the cot
The poor man sits, with all his fam'ly round,
In awful expectation of thy sound.
Lone on his way the trav'ller stands aghast;
The fearful looks of man to heav'n are cast,
When, lo! thy lightning gleams on high,
As swiftly turns his startled eye;
And swiftly as thy shooting blaze
Each half performed motion stays,
Deep awe, all human strife and labour stills,
And thy dread voice alone, the earth and heaven fills.

   Bright bursts the lightning from the cloud's dark womb,
As quickly swallow'd in the closing gloom.
The distant streamy flashes, spread askance
In paler sheetings, skirt the wide expanse.
Dread flaming from aloft, the cat'ract dire
Oft meets in middle space the nether fire.
Fierce, red, and ragged, shiv'ring in the air,

Athwart mid-darkness shoots the lengthen'd glare.
Wild glancing round, the feebler lightning plays;
The rifted centre pours the gen'ral blaze;
And from the warring clouds in fury driven,[2]
Red writhing falls the keen embodied bolt of heaven.

From the dark bowels of the burthen'd cloud
Dread swells the rolling peal, full, deep'ning, loud.
Wide ratt'ling claps the heaven's scatter'd o'er,
In gather'd strength lift the tremendous roar;
With weaning force it rumbles over head,
Then, growling, wears away to silence dread.
Now waking from afar in doubled might,
Slow rolling onward to the middle height;
Like crash of mighty mountains downward hurl'd,
Like the upbreaking of a wrecking world,
In dreadful majesty, th' explosion grand
Bursts wide, and awful, o'er the trembling land.
The lofty mountains echo back the roar,
Deep from the afar rebounds earth's rocky shore;
All else existing in the senses bound
Is lost in the immensity of sound.
Wide jarring sounds by turns in strength convene,
And deep, and terrible, the solemn pause between.

1790

Aloft upon the mountain's side
The kindled forest blazes wide.
Huge fragments of the rugged steep
Are tumbled to the lashing deep.
Firm rooted in the cloven rock,
Loud crashing falls the stubborn oak.
The lightning keen, in wasteful ire,
Fierce darting on the lofty spire,
Wide rends in twain the ir'n-knit stone,
And stately tow'rs are lowly thrown.

Wild flames o'erscour the wide campaign,
And plough askance the hissing main.
Nor strength of man may brave the storm,

---

2 Author's note: "In poetry we have only to do with appearances; and the zig-zag lightning, commonly thought to be the thunder-bolt, is certainly firm and embodied, compared to the ordinary lightning, which takes no distinct shape at all."

Nor shelter skreen the shrinking form;
Nor castle wall its fury stay,
Nor massy gate may bar its way.
It visits those of low estate,
It shakes the dwellings of the great,
It looks athwart the secret tomb,
And glares upon the prison's gloom;
While dungeons deep, in unknown light,
Flash hidious on the wretches' sight,
And lowly groans the downward cell,
Where deadly silence wont to dwell.

Now upcast eyes to heav'n adore,
And knees that never bow'd before.
In stupid wonder stares the child;
The maiden turns her glances wild,
And lifts to hear the coming roar:
The agéd shake their locks so hoar:
And stoutest hearts begin to fail,
And many a manly cheek is pale;
Till nearer closing peals astound,
And crashing ruin mingles round;
Then 'numbing fear awhile up-binds
The pausing action of their minds,
Till wak'd to dreadful sense, they lift their eyes,
And round the stricken corse, shrill shrieks of horror rise.

Now thinly spreads the falling hail
A motly winter o'er the vale,
The hailstones bounding as they fall
On hardy rock, or storm-beat wall.
The loud beginning peal its fury checks,
Now full, now fainter, with irreg'lar breaks,
Then weak in force, unites the scatter'd sound;
And rolls its lengthen'd grumblings to the distant bound.
A thick and muddy whiteness clothes the sky,
In paler flashes gleams the lightning by;
And thro' the rent cloud, silver'd with his ray,
The sun looks down on all this wild affray;
As high enthron'd above all mortal ken,
A greater Pow'r beholds the strife of men:
Yet o'er the distant hills the darkness scowls,
And deep, and long, the parting tempest growls.

1790

14

THE BASTILLE, A VISION

Helen Maria Williams

"Drear cell! along whose lonely bounds,
Unvisited by light,
Chill silence dwells with night,
Save where the clanging fetter sounds!
Abyss, where mercy never came,
Nor hope, the wretch can find;
Where long inaction wastes the frame,
And half annihilates the mind!

Stretch'd helpless in this living tomb,
Oh haste, congenial death!
Seize, seize this ling'ring breath,
And shroud me in unconscious gloom—
Britain! thy exil'd son no more
Thy blissful vales shall see;
Why did I leave thy hallow'd shore,
Distinguish'd land, where all are free?"

1790

Bastille! within thy hideous pile,
Which stains of blood defile—
Thus rose the captive's sighs,
Till slumber seal'd his weeping eyes—
Terrific visions hover near!
He sees an awful form appear!
Who drags his step to deeper cells,
Where stranger wilder horror dwells!

"O! tear me from these haunted walls,
Or these fierce shapes controul!
Lest madness seize my soul—
That pond'rous mask of iron falls,
I see!"—"Rash mortal, ha! beware,
Nor breathe that hidden name!
Should those dire accents wound the air,
Know death shall lock thy stiff'ning frame.

Hark! that loud bell which sullen tolls!
It wakes a shriek of woe.
From yawning depths below;
Shrill through this hollow vault it rolls!
A deed was done in this black cell,
Unfit for mortal ear!
A deed was done, when toll'd that knell,
No human heart could live and hear!

Rouze thee from thy numbing trance,
Near yon thick gloom advance;
The solid cloud has shook;
Arm all thy soul with strength to look.—
Enough! thy starting locks have rose,
Thy limbs have fail'd, thy blood has froze:
On scenes so foul, with mad affright,
I fix no more thy fasten'd sight.

Those troubled phantoms melt away!
I lose the sense of care—
I feel the vital air—
I *see*, I *see* the light of day!—
Visions of bliss! eternal powers!
What force has shook those hated walls?
What arm has rent those threat'ning towers?
It falls—the guilty fabric falls!"

"Now, favour'd mortal, now behold!
To soothe thy captive state,
 I ope the book of fate,
Mark what its registers unfold!
Where this dark pile in chaos lies,
With nature's execrations hurl'd,
Shall Freedom's sacred temple rise,
And charm an emulating world!

'Tis her awak'ning voice commands
Those firm, those patriot bands,
Arm'd to avenge her cause,
And guard her violated laws!—

1790

16

Did ever earth a scene display
More glorious to the eye of day,
Than millions with according mind,
Who claim the rights of human kind?

Does the fam'd Roman page sublime,
An hour more bright unroll,
To animate the soul,
Than this, lov'd theme of future time?—
Posterity, with rev'rence meet,
The consecrated act shall hear;
Age shall the glowing tale repeat,
And youth shall drop the burning tear!

The peasant, while he fondly sees
His infants round the hearth,
Pursue their simple mirth,
Or emulously climb his knees,
No more bewails their future lot,
By tyranny's stern rod opprest;
While Freedom cheers his straw-roof'd cot,
And tells him all his toils are blest.

1790

Philosophy! oh, share the meed
Of Freedom's noblest deed!
'Tis thine each truth to scan,
Guardian of bliss, and friend of man!
'Tis thine all human wrongs to heal,
'Tis thine to love all nature's weal;
To give each gen'rous purpose birth,
And renovate the gladden'd earth."

17

1792

THE RIGHTS OF WOMAN[3]

Anna Letitia Barbauld

Yes, injured Woman! rise, assert thy right!
Woman! too long degraded, scorned, opprest;
O born to rule in partial Law's despite,
Resume thy native empire o'er the breast!

Go forth arrayed in panoply divine;
That angel pureness which admits no stain;
Go, bid proud Man his boasted rule resign,
And kiss the golden sceptre of thy reign.

Go, gird thyself with grace; collect thy store
Of bright artillery glancing from afar;
Soft melting tones thy thundering cannon's roar,
Blushes and fears thy magazine of war.

Thy rights are empire: urge no meaner claim,—
Felt, not defined, and if debated, lost;
Like sacred mysteries, which withheld from fame,
Shunning discussion, are revered the most.

Try all that wit and art suggest to bend
Of thy imperial foe the stubborn knee;
Make treacherous Man thy subject, not thy friend;
Thou mayst command, but never canst be free.

Awe the licentious, and restrain the rude;
Soften the sullen, clear the cloudy brow:
Be, more than princes' gifts, thy favours sued;—
She hazards all, who will the least allow.

But hope not, courted idol of mankind,
On this proud eminence secure to stay;
Subduing and subdued, thou soon shalt find
Thy coldness soften, and thy pride give way.

Then, then, abandon each ambitious thought,
Conquest or rule thy heart shall feebly move,
In Nature's school, by her soft maxims taught,
That separate rights are lost in mutual love.

3 Written as a reaction to Wollstonecraft's *Vindication of the Rights of Woman* (1792). Wollstonecraft had taken particular aim at Barbauld and her poem "To a Lady, with some painted flowers" (1773).

THE DEAD BEGGAR.

*AN ELEGY, ADDRESSED TO A LADY, WHO WAS
AFFECTED AT SEEING THE FUNERAL OF A NAMELESS
PAUPER, BURIED AT THE EXPENCE OF THE PARISH,
IN THE CHURCH-YARD AT BRIGHTHELMSTONE, IN
NOVEMBER 1792*

Charlotte Smith

Swells then thy feeling heart, and streams thine eye
   O'er the deserted being, poor and old,
Whom cold, reluctant, Parish Charity
   Consigns to mingle with his kindred mold?

Mourn'st thou, that *here* the time-worn sufferer ends
   Those evil days still threatening woes to come;
Here, where the friendless feel no want of friends,
   Where even the houseless wanderer finds an home!

What tho' no kindred croud in sable forth,
   And sigh, or seem to sigh, around his bier;
Tho' o'er his coffin with the humid earth
   No children drop the unavailing tear?

Rather rejoice that *here* his sorrows cease,
   Whom sickness, age, and poverty oppress'd;
Where Death, the Leveller, restores to peace
   The wretch who living knew not where to rest.

Rejoice, that tho' an outcast spurn'd by Fate,
   Thro' penury's rugged path his race he ran;
In earth's cold bosom, equall'd with the great,
   Death vindicates the insulted rights of Man.

Rejoice, that tho' severe his earthly doom,
   And rude, and sown with thorns the way he trod,
Now, (where unfeeling Fortune cannot come)
   He rests upon the mercies of his GOD.

1792

1793

A WISH

Samuel Rogers

Mine be a cot beside the hill;
A bee-hive's hum shall soothe my ear;
A willowy brook, that turns a mill,
With many a fall, shall linger near.

The swallow, oft, beneath my thatch,
Shall twitter from her clay-built nest;
Oft shall the pilgrim lift the latch,
And share my meal, a welcome guest.

Around my ivied porch shall spring
Each fragrant flower that drinks the dew;
And Lucy, at her wheel, shall sing,
In russet gown and apron blue.

The village church, among the trees,
Where first our marriage-vows were giv'n,
With merry peals shall swell the breeze,
And point the taper spire to heav'n.

THE ALPS AT DAYBREAK

Samuel Rogers

The sun-beams streak the azure skies,
And line with light the mountain's brow:
With hounds and horns the hunters rise,
And chase the roebuck thro' the snow.

From rock to rock, with giant bound,
High on their iron poles they pass;
Mute, lest the air, convuls'd by sound,
Rend from above a frozen mass.

The goats wind slow their wonted way,
Up craggy steeps and ridges rude;
Mark'd by the wild wolf for his prey,
From desert cave or hanging wood.

And while the torrent thunders loud,
And as the echoing cliffs reply,
The huts peep o'er the morning cloud,
Perch'd, like an eagle's nest, on high.

from THE EMIGRANTS (BOOK II)
Charlotte Smith

SCENE, *on an Eminence on one of those Downs, which afford to the South a View of the Sea; to the North of the Weald of Sussex.*

TIME, *an Afternoon in April, 1793.*

Long wintry months are past; the Moon that now
Lights her pale crescent even at noon, has made
Four times her revolution; since with step,
Mournful and slow, along the wave-worn cliff,
Pensive I took my solitary way,
Lost in despondence, while contemplating
Not my own wayward destiny alone,
(Hard as it is, and difficult to bear!)
But in beholding the unhappy lot
Of the lorn Exiles; who, amid the storms
Of wild disastrous Anarchy, are thrown,
Like shipwreck'd sufferers, on England's coast,
To see, perhaps, no more their native land,
Where Desolation riots: They, like me,
From fairer hopes and happier prospects driven,
Shrink from the future, and regret the past.
But on this Upland scene, while April comes,
With fragrant airs, to fan my throbbing breast,
Fain would I snatch an interval from Care,
That weighs my wearied spirit down to earth;
Courting, once more, the influence of Hope

1793

(For "Hope" still waits upon the flowery prime)
As here I mark Spring's humid hand unfold
The early leaves that fear capricious winds,
While, even on shelter'd banks, the timid flowers
Give, half reluctantly, their warmer hues
To mingle with the primroses' pale stars.
No shade the leafless copses yet afford,
Nor hide the mossy labours of the Thrush,
That, startled, darts across the narrow path;
But quickly re-assur'd, resumes his task,
Or adds his louder notes to those that rise
From yonder tufted brake; where the white buds
Of the first thorn are mingled with the leaves
Of that which blossoms on the brow of May.

    Ah! 'twill not be:—So many years have pass'd,
Since, on my native hills, I learn'd to gaze
On these delightful landscapes; and those years
Have taught me so much sorrow, that my soul
Feels not the joy reviving Nature brings;
But, in dark retrospect, dejected dwells
On human follies, and on human woes.—
What is the promise of the infant year,
The lively verdure, or the bursting blooms,
To those, who shrink from horrors such as War
Spreads o'er the affrighted world? With swimming eye,
Back on the past they throw their mournful looks,
And see the Temple, which they fondly hop'd
Reason would raise to Liberty, destroy'd
By ruffian hands; while, on the ruin'd mass,
Flush'd with hot blood, the Fiend of Discord sits
In savage triumph; mocking every plea
Of policy and justice, as she shews
The headless corse of one, whose only crime
Was being born a Monarch—Mercy turns,
From spectacle so dire, her swol'n eyes;
And Liberty, with calm, unruffled brow
Magnanimous, as conscious of her strength
In Reason's panoply, scorns to distain
Her righteous cause with carnage, and resigns
To Fraud and Anarchy the infuriate crowd.—

1793

22

SCOTS WHA HAE WI' WALLACE BLED

Robert Burns

Scots, wha hae wi' Wallace bled,
Scots, wham Bruce has aften led;
Welcome to your gory bed,
    Or tae victorie!

Now's the day, and now's the hour;
See the front o' battle lour:
See approach proud Edward's pow'r—
    Chains and slaverie!

Wha will be a traitor knave?
Wha can fill a coward's grave?
Wha sae base as be a slave?
    Let him turn and flee!

Wha for Scotland's King and law
Freedom's sword will strongly draw,
Freeman stand, or freeman fa',
    Let him follow me!

By oppression's woes and pains,
By your sons in servile chains,
We will drain our dearest veins,
    But they shall be free!

Lay the proud usurpers low!
Tyrants fall in every foe!
Liberty's in every blow!—
    Let us do or die!

1793

1794

From **SONGS OF EXPERIENCE**
William Blake

INTRODUCTION

Hear the voice of the Bard!
Who Present, Past, & Future sees
Whose ears have heard,
The Holy Word,
That walk'd among the ancient trees.

Calling the lapsed Soul
And weeping in the evening dew;
That might controll,
The starry pole;
And fallen fallen light renew!

O Earth O Earth return!
Arise from out the dewy grass;
Night is worn,
And the morn
Rises from the slumberous mass.

Turn away no more:
Why wilt thou turn away
The starry floor
The watry shore
Is giv'n thee till the break of day.

THE CLOD & THE PEBBLE
William Blake

Love seeketh not itself to please,
Nor for itself hath any care;
But for another gives its ease,
And builds a Heaven in Hells despair.

So sung a little Clod of Clay
Trodden with the cattle's feet,

But a Pebble of the brook
Warbled out these metres meet:

Love seeketh only Self to please,
To bind another to its delight,
Joys in anothers loss of ease,
And builds a Hell in Heavens despite.

HOLY THURSDAY
William Blake

Is this a holy thing to see,
In a rich and fruitful land,
Babes reducd to misery,
Fed with cold and usurous hand?

Is that trembling cry a song?
Can it be a song of joy?
And so many children poor?
It is a land of poverty!

And their sun does never shine.
And their fields are bleak & bare.
And their ways are fill'd with thorns.
It is eternal winter there.

For where-e'er the sun does shine,
And where-e'er the rain does fall:
Babe can never hunger there,
Nor poverty the mind appall.

1794

THE CHIMNEY SWEEPER
William Blake

A little black thing among the snow,
Crying weep, weep, in notes of woe!
Where are thy father & mother? say?
They are both gone up to the church to pray.
Because I was happy upon the heath,
And smil'd among the winter's snow:
They clothed me in the clothes of death,
And taught me to sing the notes of woe.

And because I am happy & dance & sing,
They think they have done me no injury:
And are gone to praise God & his Priest & King,
Who make up a heaven of our misery.

THE TYGER
William Blake

Tyger Tyger, burning bright,
In the forests of the night;
What immortal hand or eye,
Could frame thy fearful symmetry?

In what distant deeps or skies.
Burnt the fire of thine eyes?
On what wings dare he aspire?
What the hand, dare sieze the fire?

And what shoulder, & what art,
Could twist the sinews of thy heart?
And when thy heart began to beat,
What dread hand? & what dread feet?

1794

What the hammer? what the chain,
In what furnace was thy brain?
What the anvil? what dread grasp,
Dare its deadly terrors clasp!

When the stars threw down their spears
And water'd heaven with their tears:
Did he smile his work to see?
Did he who made the Lamb make thee?

Tyger Tyger burning bright,
In the forests of the night:
What immortal hand or eye,
Dare frame thy fearful symmetry?

LONDON
William Blake

I wander thro' each charter'd street,
Near where the charter'd Thames does flow.
And mark in every face I meet
Marks of weakness, marks of woe.

In every cry of every Man,
In every Infants cry of fear,
In every voice: in every ban,
The mind-forg'd manacles I hear

How the Chimney-sweepers cry
Every blackning Church appalls,
And the hapless Soldiers sigh
Runs in blood down Palace walls

But most thro' midnight streets I hear
How the youthful Harlots curse
Blasts the new-born Infants tear
And blights with plagues the Marriage hearse

IT WAS A' FOR OUR RIGHTFUL KING

Robert Burns

It was a' for our rightful king
     That we left fair Scotland's strand;
It was a' for our rightful king
     We e'er saw Irish land, my dear,
     We e'er saw Irish land.

1794

Now a' is done that men can do,
     And a' is done in vain:
My Love, and Native Land, fareweel,
     For I maun cross the main, my dear,
     For I maun cross the main.

He turn'd him right and round about,
     Upon the Irish shore,
He gae his bridle reins a shake,
     With, adieu for evermore, my dear!
     And adieu for evermore!

The soger frae the war returns,
     And the sailor frae the main.
But I hae parted frae my Love,
     Never to meet again, my dear,
     Never to meet again.

When day is gane and night is come,
    And a' folk bound to sleep;
I think on him that's far awa
    The lee-lang night, and weep, my dear,
    The lee-lang night, and weep.

THE PAUPER'S FUNERAL
Robert Southey

What! and not one to heave the pious sigh!
Not one whose sorrow-swoln and aching eye
For social scenes, for life's endearments fled,
Shall drop a tear and dwell upon the dead!
Poor wretched Outcast! I will weep for thee,
And sorrow for forlorn humanity.
Yes, I will weep; but not that thou art come
To the stern sabbath of the silent tomb:
For squalid Want, and the black scorpion Care,
Heart-withering fiends! shall never enter there.
I sorrow for the ills thy life has known
As thro' the world's long pilgrimage, alone,
Haunted by Poverty and woe-begone,
Unloved, unfriended, thou didst journey on:
Thy youth in ignorance and labour past,
And thine old age all barrenness and blast!
Hard was thy Fate, which, while it doom'd to woe,
Denied thee wisdom to support the blow;
And robb'd of all its energy thy mind,
Ere yet it cast thee on thy fellow-kind,
Abject of thought, the victim of distress,
To wander in the world's wide wilderness.

Poor Outcast sleep in peace! the wintry storm
Blows bleak no more on thine unshelter'd form;
Thy woes are past; thou restest in the tomb;—
I pause—and ponder on the days to come.

1794

1795

HYMN, IMITATED FROM THE FRENCH[4]
Helen Maria Williams

Calm all the tumults that invade
Our souls, and lend Thy pow'rful aid.
O Source of Mercy! soothe our pains,
And break, O break our cruel chains!
To Thee the captive pours his cry,
To Thee the mourner loves to fly;
The incense of our tears receive,
'Tis all the incense we can give.
Eternal Power, our cause defend,
O God! of innocence the friend!
Near Thee for ever she resides,
In Thee for ever she confides;
Thou know'st the secrets of the breast,
Thou know'st th' oppressor and th' opprest;
Do Thou our wrongs with pity see,
Avert a doom offending Thee!
But should the murd'rer's arm prevail,
Should tyranny our lives assail,
Unmov'd, triumphant, scorning death,
We'll bless Thee with our latest breath!—
The hour, the glorious hour will come,
That consecrates the patriot's tomb;
And, with the pang our mem'ry claims,
Our country will avenge our names.

1795

---

4 Author's note: "This little Hymn was composed by M. La Source,
during the reign of terror, in the prison of the Luxembourg, and
was usually sung by him and the Marquis de Sillery every evening,
in our apartment of the prison, to which they constantly repaired
for a few hours after having passed the day on their trial before the
Revolutionary Tribunal. This simple dirge, which was adapted to
a soft solemn air, and sung in a low tone, they called their evening
service. Those mournful sounds, the knell of my departing friends,
yet thrill upon my heart! They were soon after dragged to the
scaffold, with the illustrious members of the Gironde, the martyrs of
their country."

INSCRIPTION FOR AN ICE HOUSE
Anna Laetitia Barbauld

Stranger, approach! within this iron door
Thrice locked and bolted, this rude arch beneath
That vaults with ponderous stone the cell; confined
By man, the great magician, who controuls
Fire, earth and air, and genii of the storm,
And bends the most remote and opposite things
To do him service and perform his will,—
A giant sits; stern Winter; here he piles,
While summer glows around, and southern gales
Dissolve the fainting world, his treasured snows
Within the rugged cave.—Stranger, approach!
He will not cramp thy limbs with sudden age,
Nor wither with his touch the coyest flower
That decks thy scented hair. Indignant here,
Like fettered Sampson when his might was spent
In puny feats to glad the festive halls
Of Gaza's wealthy sons; or he who sat

1795

Midst laughing girls submiss, and patient twirled
The slender spindle in his sinewy grasp;

The rugged power, fair Pleasure's minister,
Exerts his art to deck the genial board;
Congeals the melting peach, the nectarine smooth,
Burnished and glowing from the sunny wall:
Darts sudden frost into the crimson veins
Of the moist berry; moulds the sugared hail:
Cools with his icy breath our flowing cups;
Or gives to the fresh dairy's nectared bowls
A quicker zest. Sullen he plies his task,
And on his shaking fingers counts the weeks
Of lingering Summer, mindful of his hour
To rush in whirlwinds forth, and rule the year.

TO THE POOR
Anna Letitia Barbauld

Child of distress, who meet'st the bitter scorn
Of fellow men to happier prospects born,

Doomed Art and Nature's various stores to see
Flow in full cups of joy—and not for thee;
Who seest the rich, to heaven and fate resign'd,
Bear *thy* afflictions with a patient mind;
Whose bursting heart disdains unjust controul,
Who feel'st oppression's iron in thy soul,
Who dragg'st the load of faint and feeble years,
Whose bread is anguish, and whose water tears;
Bear, bear thy wrongs—fulfill thy destined hour,
Bend thy meek neck beneath the foot of Power;
But when thou feel'st the great deliverer nigh,
And thy freed spirit mounting seeks the sky,
Let no vain fears thy parting hour molest,
No whispered terrors shake thy quiet breast:
Think not their threats can work thy future woe,
Nor deem the Lord above like lords below;—
Safe in the bosom of that love repose
By whom the sun gives light, the ocean flows;
Prepare to meet a Father undismayed,
Nor fear the God whom priests and kings have made.[5]

TO MARY WOLLSTONECRAFT
Robert Southey   1795

The lilly cheek, the "purple light of love,"
The liquid lustre of the melting eye,—
Mary! of these the Poet sung, for these
Did Woman triumph! with no angry frown
View this degrading conquest. At that age
No MAID OF ARC had snatch'd from coward man
The heaven-blest sword of Liberty; thy sex
Could boast no female ROLAND's martyrdom;
No CORDE's angel and avenging arm
Had sanctified again the murderer's name
As erst when Caesar perish'd: yet some strains
May even adorn this theme, befitting me
To offer, nor unworthy thy regard.

---

5 Lucy Aikin, the editor of the 1825 *The Works of Anna Laetitia Barbauld* inserted the following note: "These lines, written in 1795, were described by Mrs. B., on sending them to a friend, as 'inspired by indignation on hearing sermons in which the poor are addressed in a manner which evidently shows the design of making religion an engine of government" (I, 193).

JANUARY 1795
Mary Robinson

Pavement slipp'ry, people sneezing,
Lords in ermine, beggars freezing;
Titled gluttons dainties carving,
Genius in a garret starving.

Lofty mansions, warm and spacious;
Courtiers cringing and voracious;
Misers scarce the wretched heeding;
Gallant soldiers fighting, bleeding.

Wives who laugh at passive spouses;
Theatres, and meeting-houses;
Balls, where simp'ring misses languish;
Hospitals, and groans of anguish.

Arts and sciences bewailing;
Commerce drooping, credit failing;
Placemen mocking subjects loyal;
Separations, weddings royal.

Authors who can't earn a dinner;
Many a subtle rogue a winner;
Fugitives for shelter seeking;
Misers hoarding, tradesmen breaking.

Taste and talents quite deserted;
All the laws of truth perverted;
Arrogance o'er merit soaring;
Merit silently deploring.

Ladies gambling night and morning;
Fools the works of genius scorning;
Ancient dames for girls mistaken,
Youthful damsels quite forsaken.

Some in luxury delighting;
More in talking than in fighting;
Lovers old, and beaux decrepid;
Lordlings empty and insipid.

1795

Poets, painters, and musicians;
Lawyers, doctors, politicians:
Pamphlets, newspapers, and odes,
Seeking fame by diff'rent roads.

Gallant souls with empty purses;
Gen'rals only fit for nurses;
School-boys, smit with martial spirit,
Taking place of vet'ran merit.

Honest men who can't get places,
Knaves who shew unblushing faces;
Ruin hasten'd, peace retarded;
Candor spurn'd, and art rewarded.

THE RIOT;
OR HALF A LOAF IS BETTER THAN NO BREAD

IN A DIALOGUE BETWEEN JACK ANVIL AND TOM HOD.
TO THE TUNE OF —"A COBBLER THERE WAS" [WRITTEN
IN NINETY-FIVE, A YEAR OF SCARCITY AND ALARM]

Hannah More

1795

TOM
Come neighbours, no longer be patient and quiet,
Come let us go kick up a bit of a riot;
I'm hungry, my lads, but I've little to eat,
So we'll pull down the mills, and we'll seize all the meat:
I'll give you good sport, boys, as ever you saw,
So a fig for the justice, a fig for the law.
                              Derry down.

Then his pitchfork Tom seized—Hold a moment, says Jack,
I'll show thee thy blunder, brave boy, in a crack,
And if I don't prove we had better be still,
I'll assist thee straightway to pull down every mill;
I'll show thee how passion thy reason does cheat,
Or I'll join thee in plunder for bread and for meat.
                              Derry down.

What a whimsey to think thus our bellies to fill,
For we stop all the grinding by breaking the mill!

33

What a whimsey to think we shall get more to eat
By abusing the butchers who get us the meat!
What a whimsey to think we shall mend our spare diet
By breeding disturbance, by murder, and riot!
                              Derry down.

Because I am dry, 'twould be foolish, I think,
To pull out my tap, and to spill all my drink;
Because I am hungry and want to be fed,
That is sure no wise reason for wasting my bread:
And just such wise reasons for mending their diet
Are used by those blockheads who rush into riot.
                              Derry down.

I would not take comfort from others' distresses,
But still I would mark how God our land blesses;
For though in Old England the times are but sad,
Abroad, I am told, they are ten times as bad;
In the land of the pope there is scarce any grain,
And 'tis worse still, they say, both in Holland and Spain.
                              Derry down.

1795   Let us look to the harvest our wants to beguile,
See the lands with rich crops how they every where smile!
Meantime to assist us, by each western breeze,
Some corn is brought daily across the salt seas!
Of tea we'll drink little, of gin none at all,
And we'll patiently wait, and the prices will fall.
                              Derry down.

But if we're not quiet, then let us not wonder
If things grow much worse by our riot and plunder;
And let us remember whenever we meet,
The more ale we drink, boys, the less we shall eat.
On those days spent in riot, no bread you brought home;
Had you spent them in labour, you must have had some.
                              Derry down.

A dinner of herbs, says the wise man, with quiet,
Is better than beef amid discord and riot.
If the thing could be help'd, I'm a foe to all strife,
And I pray for a peace every night of my life;
But in matters of state not an inch will I budge,
Because I conceive I'm no very good judge.
                              Derry down.

But though poor, I can work, my brave boy, with the best,
Let the king and the parliament manage the rest;
I lament both the war and the taxes together,
Though I verily think they don't alter the weather.
The king, as I take it, with very good reason,
May prevent a bad law, but can't help a bad season.
Derry down.

The parliament men, although great is their power,
Yet they cannot contrive us a bit of a shower;
And I never yet heard, though our rulers are wise,
That they know very well how to manage the skies;
For the best of them all, as they found to their cost
Were not able to hinder last winter's hard frost.
Derry down.

Besides I must share in the wants of the times,
Because I have had my full share in its crimes;
And I'm apt to believe the distress which is sent,
Is to punish and cure us of all discontent.
But harvest is coming—potatoes are come!
Our prospect clears up; ye complainers, be dumb!
Derry down.

1795

And though I've no money, and though I've no lands,
I've head on my should, and a pair of good hands;
So I'll work the whole day, and on Sundays I'll seek
At church how to bear all the wants of the week.
The gentlefolks too will afford us supplies,
They'll subscribe—and they'll give up their puddings and pies.
Derry down.

Then before I'm induced to take part in a riot,
I'll ask this short question—What shall I get by it?
So I'll e'en wait a little, till cheaper the bread,
For a mittimus hangs o'er each rioter's head;
And when of two evils I'm ask'd which is best,
I'd rather be hungry than hang'd, I protest.
Derry down.

Quoth Tom, thou are right; if I rise, I'm a Turk;
So he threw down his pitchfork, and went to his work.

1796

POEMS ON THE SLAVE TRADE - SONNET III
Robert Southey

Oh he is worn with toil! the big drops run
  Down his dark cheek; hold—hold thy merciless hand,
  Pale tyrant! for beneath thy hard command
O'er wearied Nature sinks. The scorching Sun,
As pityless as proud Prosperity,
  Darts on him his full beams; gasping he lies
  Arraigning with his looks the patient skies,
While that inhuman trader lifts on high
  The mangling scourge. Oh ye who at your ease
  Sip the blood-sweeten'd beverage! thoughts like these
Haply ye scorn: I thank thee Gracious God!
  That I do feel upon my cheek the glow
Of indignation, when beneath the rod
  A sable brother writhes in silent woe.

1796

THE GRANDAME
Charles Lamb

             On the green hill-top,
Hard by the house of prayer, a modest roof,
And not distinguish'd from its neighbour barn,
Save by a slender-tapering length of spire,
The Grandame sleeps: a plain stone barely tells
The name and date to the chance passenger.
For lowly born was she, and long had eat
Well-earn'd, the bread of service:—hers was else
A mountain spirit, one that entertain'd
Scorn of base action, deed dishonorable,
Or aught unseemly. I remember well
Her reverend image: I remember too,
With what a zeal she serv'd her Master's house;
And how the prattling tongue of garrulous age
Delighted to recount the oft-told tale

Or anecdote domestic. Wise she was,
And wondrous skill'd in genealogies,
And could in apt and voluble terms discourse
Of births, of titles, and alliances;
Of marriages, and intermarriages;
Relationship remote, or near of kin;
Of friends offended, family disgraced,
Maiden high-born, but wayward, disobeying
Parental strict injunctions, and regardless
Of unmix'd blood, and ancestry remote,
Stooping to wed with one of low degree.
But these are not thy praises; and I wrong
Thy honor'd memory, recording chiefly
Things light or trivial. Better 'twere to tell,
How with a nobler zeal, and warmer love,
She served her *heavenly Master*. I have seen
That reverend form bent down with age and pain,
And rankling malady: yet not for this
Ceas'd she to praise her Maker, or withdrew
Her trust in Him, her faith, an humble hope—
So meekly had she learn'd to bear her cross—
For she had studied patience in the school
Of Christ; much comfort she had thence derived,
And was a follower of the NAZARENE.

1796

1797

ON BEING CAUTIONED AGAINST WALKING ON AN HEADLAND OVERLOOKING THE SEA, BECAUSE IT WAS FREQUENTED BY A LUNATIC
Charlotte Smith

Is there a solitary wretch who hies
   To the tall cliff, with starting pace or slow,
And, measuring, views with wild and hollow eyes
   Its distance from the waves that chide below;
Who, as the sea-born gale with frequent sighs
   Chills his cold bed upon the mountain turf,
With hoarse, half-utter'd lamentation, lies
   Murmuring responses to the dashing surf?
In moody sadness, on the giddy brink,
   I see him more with envy than with fear;
He has no *nice felicities* that shrink
   From giant horrors; wildly wandering here,
He seems (uncursed with reason) not to know
The depth or the duration of his woe.

1797

WASHING DAY
Anna Laetitia Barbauld

"...and their voice,
Turning again towards childish treble, pipes
And whistles in its sound."[6]

The Muses are turned gossips; they have lost
The buskin'd step, and clear high-sounding phrase,
Language of gods. Come, then, domestic Muse,

In slip-shod measure loosely prattling on,
Of farm or orchard, pleasant curds and cream,
Or drowning flies, or shoe lost in the mire
By little whimpering boy, with rueful face;
Come, Muse, and sing the dreaded *Washing-Day*.

6 From Shakespeare's *As You Like It*. In Act II, Jaques describes the
seven ages of man. Barbauld has changed "his" to "their."

—Ye who beneath the yoke of wedlock bend,
With bowed soul, full well ye ken the day
Which week, smooth sliding after week, brings on
Too soon; for to that day nor peace belongs,
Nor comfort; e'er the first grey streak of dawn,
The red-arm'd washers come and chase repose.
Nor pleasant smile, nor quaint device of mirth,
E'er visited that day; the very cat,
From the wet kitchen scared, and reeking hearth,
Visits the parlour, an unwonted guest.
The silent breakfast meal is soon dispatch'd
Uninterrupted, save by anxious looks
Cast at the lowering sky, if sky should lower.
From that last evil, oh preserve us, heavens!
For should the skies pour down, adieu to all
Remains of quiet; then expect to hear
Of sad disasters—dirt and gravel stains
Hard to efface, and loaded lines at once
Snapped short—and linen-horse by dog thrown down,
And all the petty miseries of life.
Saints have been calm while stretched upon the rack,
And Montezuma smil'd on burning coals;
But never yet did housewife notable

1797

Greet with a smile a rainy washing-day.
—But grant the welkin fair, require not thou
Who call'st thyself perchance the master there,
Or study swept, or nicely dusted coat,
Or usual 'tendance; ask not, indiscreet,
Thy stockings mended, tho' the yawning rents
Gape wide as Erebus; nor hope to find
Some snug recess impervious; should'st thou try
The 'customed garden walks, thine eye shall rue
The budding fragrance of thy tender shrubs,
Myrtle or rose, all crushed beneath the weight
Of coarse check'd apron, with impatient hand
Twitch'd off when showers impend; or crossing lines
Shall mar thy musings, as the wet cold sheet
Flaps in thy face abrupt. Woe to the friend
Whose evil stars have urged him forth to claim
On such a day the hospitable rites;

Looks, blank at best, and stinted courtesy,
Shall he receive; vainly he feeds his hopes
With dinner of roast chicken, savoury pie,
Or tart or pudding:—pudding he nor tart
That day shall eat; nor, tho' the husband try,
Mending what can't be help'd, to kindle mirth
From cheer deficient, shall his consort's brow
Clear up propitious; the unlucky guest
In silence dines, and early slinks away.
    I well remember, when a child, the awe
This day struck into me; for then the maids,
I scarce knew why, looked cross, and drove me from them;
Nor soft caress could I obtain, nor hope
Usual indulgencies; jelly or creams,
Relique of costly suppers, and set by
For me their petted one; or butter'd toast,
When butter was forbid; or thrilling tale
Of ghost, or witch, or murder—so I went
And shelter'd me beside the parlour fire,
There my dear grandmother, eldest of forms,
Tended the little ones, and watched from harm;

1797

Anxiously fond, though oft her spectacles
With elfin cunning hid, and oft the pins
Drawn from her ravell'd stocking, might have sour'd
One less indulgent.—
At intervals my mother's voice was heard,
Urging dispatch; briskly the work went on,
All hands employed to wash, to rinse, to wring,
Or fold, and starch, and clap, and iron, and plait.
Then would I sit me down, and ponder much
Why washings were. Sometimes thro' hollow hole
Of pipe amused we blew, and sent aloft
The floating bubbles, little dreaming then
To see, Montgolfier, thy silken ball
Ride buoyant thro' the clouds—so near approach
The sports of children and the toils of men.
Earth, air, and sky, and ocean, hath its bubbles,
And verse is one of them—this most of all.

THIS LIME-TREE BOWER MY PRISON
[ADDRESSED TO CHARLES LAMB, OF THE INDIA
HOUSE, LONDON]
Samuel Taylor Coleridge

In the June of 1797 some long-expected friends paid a visit to the
author's cottage; and on the morning of their arrival, he met with an
accident, which disabled him from walking during the whole time of
their stay. One evening, when they had left him for a few hours, he
composed the following lines in the garden-bower. [Coleridge's note]

Well, they are gone, and here must I remain,
This lime-tree bower my prison! I have lost
Beauties and feelings, such as would have been
Most sweet to my remembrance, e'en when age
Had dimm'd mine eyes to blindness! They, meanwhile,
Friends, whom I never more may meet again,
On springy heath, along the hill-top edge,
Wander in gladness, and wind down, perchance,
To that still roaring dell, of which I told:
The roaring dell, o'erwooded, narrow, deep,
And only speckled by the mid-day sun;
Where its slim trunk the ash from rock to rock
Flings arching like a bridge;—that branchless ash,
Unsunn'd and damp, whose few poor yellow leaves
Ne'er tremble in the gale, yet tremble still,
Fann'd by the water-fall! and there my friends
Behold the dark green file of long lank weeds,
That all at once (a most fantastic sight!)
Still nod and drip beneath the dripping edge
Of the blue clay-stone.

              Now, my friends emerge
Beneath the wide, wide heaven—and view again
The many-steepled tract magnificent
Of hilly fields and meadows, and the sea,
With some fair bark, perhaps, whose sails light up
The slip of smooth clear blue betwixt two isles
Of purple shadow! Yes, they wander on
In gladness all; but thou, methinks, most glad,
My gentle-hearted Charles; for thou hast pined
And hunger'd after nature, many a year,
In the great city pent, winning thy way
With sad yet patient soul, through evil and pain
And strange calamity! Ah! slowly sink

1797

Behind the western ridge, thou glorious sun!
Shine in the slant beams of the sinking orb,
Ye purple heath-flowers! richlier burn, ye clouds!
Live in the yellow light, ye distant groves!
And kindle, thou blue ocean! So my friend,
Struck with deep joy, may stand, as I have stood,
Silent with swimming sense; yea, gazing round
On the wide landscape, gaze till all doth seem
Less gross than bodily; and of such hues
As veil th' Almighty Spirit, when yet he makes
Spirits perceive his presence.
                                        A delight
Comes sudden on my heart, and I am glad
As I myself were there! Nor in this bower,
This little lime-tree bower, have I not mark'd
Much that has sooth'd me. Pale beneath the blaze
Hung the transparent foliage; and I watch'd
Some broad and sunny leaf, and lov'd to see
The shadow of the leaf, and stem above
Dappling its sunshine! And that walnut-tree
Was richly ting'd, and a deep radiance lay
Full on the ancient ivy, which usurps
Those fronting elms, and now, with blackest mass

1797

Makes their dark branches gleam a lighter hue
Through the late twilight: and though now the bat
Wheels silent by, and not a swallow twitters,
Yet still the solitary humble-bee
Sings in the bean-flower! Henceforth I shall know
That Nature ne'er deserts the wise and pure:
No plot so narrow, be but Nature there,
No waste so vacant, but may well employ
Each faculty of sense, and keep the heart
Awake to Love and Beauty! and sometimes
'Tis well to be bereft of promis'd good,
That we may lift the soul, and contemplate
With lively joy the joys we cannot share.
My gentle-hearted Charles! when the last rook
Beat its straight path along the dusky air
Homewards, I blest it! deeming its black wing
(Now a dim speck, now vanishing in light)
Had cross'd the mighty orb's dilated glory,
While thou stood'st gazing; or, when all was still,
Flew creaking o'er thy head, and had a charm
For thee, my gentle-hearted Charles, to whom
No sound is dissonant which tells of Life.

KUBLA KHAN
Or, a vision in a dream. A Fragment.

Samuel Taylor Coleridge

In Xanadu did Kubla Khan
A stately pleasure-dome decree:
Where Alph, the sacred river, ran
Through caverns measureless to man
   Down to a sunless sea.
So twice five miles of fertile ground
With walls and towers were girdled round:
And there were gardens bright with sinuous rills
Where blossomed many an incense-bearing tree;
And here were forests ancient as the hills,
Enfolding sunny spots of greenery.

But oh! that deep romantic chasm which slanted
Down the green hill athwart a cedarn cover!
A savage place! as holy and enchanted
As e'er beneath a waning moon was haunted
By woman wailing for her demon-lover!
And from this chasm, with ceaseless turmoil seething,
As if this earth in fast thick pants were breathing,
A mighty fountain momently was forced:
Amid whose swift half-intermitted burst
Huge fragments vaulted like rebounding hail,
Or chaffy grain beneath the thresher's flail:
And mid these dancing rocks at once and ever
It flung up momently the sacred river.
Five miles meandering with a mazy motion
Through wood and dale the sacred river ran,
Then reached the caverns measureless to man,
And sank in tumult to a lifeless ocean:
And 'mid this tumult Kubla heard from far
Ancestral voices prophesying war!

   The shadow of the dome of pleasure
   Floated midway on the waves;
   Where was heard the mingled measure
   From the fountain and the caves.

1797

43

It was a miracle of rare device,
A sunny pleasure-dome with caves of ice!

A damsel with a dulcimer
In a vision once I saw:
It was an Abyssinian maid,
And on her dulcimer she played,
Singing of Mount Abora.
Could I revive within me
Her symphony and song,
To such a deep delight 'twould win me,
That with music loud and long,
I would build that dome in air,
That sunny dome! those caves of ice!
And all who heard should see them there,
And all should cry, Beware! Beware!
His flashing eyes, his floating hair!
Weave a circle round him thrice,
And close your eyes with holy dread,
For he on honey-dew hath fed,
And drunk the milk of Paradise.

1797

TO MR. S.T. COLERIDGE
Anna Letitia Barbauld

Midway the hill of Science, after steep
And rugged paths that tire the unpractised feet,
A *grove* extends; in tangled mazes wrought,
And filled with strange enchantment:—dubious shapes
Flit through dim glades, and lure the eager foot
Of youthful ardour to eternal chase.
Dreams hang on every leaf; unearthly forms
Glide through the gloom, and mystic visions swim
Before the cheated sense. Athwart the mists,
Far into vacant space, huge shadows stretch
And seem realities; while things of life,
Obvious to sight and touch, all glowing round
Fade to the hue of shadows.—*Scruples* here
With filmy net, most like the autumnal webs
Of floating gossamer, arrest the foot

Of generous enterprise; and palsy hope
And fair ambition with the chilling touch
Of sickly hesitation and blank fear.
Nor seldom *Indolence*, these lawns among,
Fixes her turf-built seat; and wears the garb
Of deep philosophy, and museful sits,
In dreamy twilight of the vacant mind,
Soothed by the whispering shade; for soothing soft
The shades; and vistas lengthening into air,
With moon-beam rainbows tinted.—Here each mind
Of finer mould, acute and delicate,
In its high progress to eternal truth
Rests for a space, in fairy bowers entranced;
And loves the softened light and tender gloom;
And, pampered with most unsubstantial food,
Looks down indignant on the grosser world,
And matter's cumbrous shapings. Youth beloved
Of science—of the Muse beloved, not here,
Not in the maze of metaphysic lore
Build thou thy place of resting! lightly tread
The dangerous ground, on noble aims intent;
And be this Circe of the studious cell
Enjoyed, but still subservient. Active scenes
Shall soon with healthful spirit brace thy mind:
And fair exertion, for bright fame sustained,
For friends, for country, chase each spleen-fed fog
That blots the wide creation—
Now heaven conduct thee with a parent's love!

1797

1798

WE ARE SEVEN

William Wordsworth

A simple child, dear brother Jim,
That lightly draws its breath,
And feels its life in every limb,
What should it know of death?

I met a little cottage girl,
She was eight years old, she said;
Her hair was thick with many a curl
That cluster'd round her head.

She had a rustic, woodland air,
And she was wildly clad;
Her eyes were fair, and very fair,
—Her beauty made me glad.

1798

"Sisters and brothers, little maid,
How many may you be?"
"How many? seven in all," she said,
And wondering looked at me.

"And where are they, I pray you tell?"
She answered, "Seven are we;
And two of us at Conway dwell,
And two are gone to sea.

Two of us in the church-yard lie,
My sister and my brother,
And, in the church-yard cottage, I
Dwell near them with my mother."

"You say that two at Conway dwell,
And two are gone to sea,
Yet you are seven! I pray you tell,
Sweet Maid, how this may be?"

Then did the little Maid reply,
"Seven boys and girls are we;
Two of us in the church-yard lie,
Beneath the church-yard tree."

"You run about, my little maid,
Your limbs they are alive;
If two are in the church-yard laid,
Then ye are only five."

"Their graves are green, they may be seen,"
The little Maid replied,
"Twelve steps or more from my mother's door,
And they are side by side.

My stockings there I often knit,
My 'kerchief there I hem;
And there upon the ground I sit—
I sit and sing to them.

And often after sunset, Sir,
When it is light and fair,
I take my little porringer,
And eat my supper there.

The first that died was little Jane;
In bed she moaning lay,
Till God released her of her pain,
And then she went away.

So in the church-yard she was laid,
And all the summer dry,
Together round her grave we played,
My brother John and I.

And when the ground was white with snow,
And I could run and slide,
My brother John was forced to go,
And he lies by her side."

"How many are you, then," said I,
"If they two are in Heaven?"
The little Maiden did reply,
"O Master! we are seven."

"But they are dead; those two are dead!
Their spirits are in heaven!"
'Twas throwing words away; for still
The little Maid would have her will,
And said, "Nay, we are seven!"

1798

THE TABLES TURNED

William Wordsworth

Up! up! My friend, and clear your looks,
Why all this toil and trouble?
Up! up! my friend, and quit your books,
Or surely you'll grow double.

The sun above the mountain's head,
A freshening lustre mellow,
Through all the long green fields has spread,
His first sweet evening yellow.

Books! 'tis a dull and endless strife,
Come, hear the woodland linnet,
How sweet his music; on my life
There's more of wisdom in it.

And hark! how blithe the throstle sings!
And he is no mean preacher;
Come forth into the light of things,
Let Nature be your teacher.

1798

She has a world of ready wealth,
Our minds and hearts to bless—
Spontaneous wisdom breathed by health,
Truth breathed by chearfulness.

One impulse from a vernal wood
May teach you more of man;
Of moral evil and of good,
Than all the sages can.

Sweet is the lore which Nature brings;
Our meddling intellect
Misshapes the beauteous forms of things;
—We murder to dissect.

Enough of science and of art;
Close up these barren leaves;
Come forth, and bring with you a heart
That watches and receives.

LINES WRITTEN A FEW MILES ABOVE TINTERN ABBEY, ON REVISITING THE BANKS OF THE WYE DURING A TOUR, JULY 13, 1798

William Wordsworth

Five years have pased; five summers, with the length
Of five long winters! and again I hear
These waters, rolling from their mountain-springs
With a sweet inland murmur.—Once again
Do I behold these steep and lofty cliffs,
Which on a wild secluded scene impress
Thoughts of more deep seclusion; and connect
The landscape with the quiet of the sky.
The day is come when I again repose
Here, under this dark sycamore, and view
These plots of cottage-ground, these orchard-tufts,
Which, at this season, with their unripe fruits,
Among the woods and copses lose themselves,
Nor, with their green and simple hue, disturb
The wild green landscape. Once again I see
These hedge-rows, hardly hedge-rows, little lines
Of sportive wood run wild; these pastoral farms
Green to the very door; and wreathes of smoke
Sent up, in silence, from among the trees,
And the low copses—coming from the trees
With some uncertain notice, as might seem,
Of vagrant dwellers in the houseless woods,
Or of some hermit's cave, where by his fire
The hermit sits alone.

                Though absent long,
These forms of beauty have not been to me,
As is a landscape to a blind man's eye:
But oft, in lonely rooms, and mid the din
Of towns and cities, I have owed to them,
In hours of weariness, sensations sweet,
Felt in the blood, and felt along the heart,
And passing even into my purer mind
With tranquil restoration:—feelings too
Of unremembered pleasure; such, perhaps,
As may have no trivial influence

1798

On that best portion of a good man's life;
His little, nameless, unremembered acts
Of kindness and of love. Nor less, I trust,
To them I may have owed another gift,
Of aspect more sublime; that blessed mood,
In which the burthen of the mystery,
In which the heavy and the weary weight
Of all this unintelligible world
Is lighten'd:—that serene and blessed mood,
In which the affections gently lead us on,
Until, the breath of this corporeal frame,
And even the motion of our human blood
Almost suspended, we are laid asleep
In body, and become a living soul:
While with an eye made quiet by the power
Of harmony, and the deep power of joy,
We see into the life of things.

                    If this
Be but a vain belief, yet, oh! how oft,
In darkness, and amid the many shapes
Of joyless day-light; when the fretful stir
Unprofitable, and the fever of the world,
Have hung upon the beatings of my heart,
How oft, in spirit, have I turned to thee,
O sylvan Wye! Thou wanderer through the woods,
How often has my spirit turned to thee!

And now, with gleams of half-extinguish'd thought,
With many recognitions dim and faint,
And somewhat of a sad perplexity,
The picture of the mind revives again:
While here I stand, not only with the sense
Of present pleasure, but with pleasing thoughts
That in this moment there is life and food
For future years. And so I dare to hope
Though changed, no doubt, from what I was, when first
I came among these hills; when like a roe
I bounded o'er the mountains, by the sides
Of the deep rivers, and the lonely streams,
Wherever nature led; more like a man
Flying from something that he dreads, than one
Who sought the thing he loved. For nature then
(The coarser pleasures of my boyish days,

1798

And their glad animal movements all gone by,)
To me was all in all.—I cannot paint
What then I was. The sounding cataract
Haunted me like a passion: the tall rock,
The mountain, and the deep and gloomy wood,
Their colours and their forms, were then to me
An appetite: a feeling and a love,
That had no need of a remoter charm,
By thought supplied, or any interest
Unborrowed from the eye.—That time is past,
And all its aching joys are now no more,
And all its dizzy raptures. Not for this
Faint I, nor mourn nor murmur: other gifts
Have followed, for such loss, I would believe,
Abundant recompence. For I have learned
To look on nature, not as in the hour
Of thoughtless youth, but hearing oftentimes
The still, sad music of humanity,
Nor harsh nor grating, though of ample power
To chasten and subdue. And I have felt
A presence that disturbs me with the joy
Of elevated thoughts; a sense sublime
Of something far more deeply interfused,
Whose dwelling is the light of setting suns, 1798
And the round ocean, and the living air,
And the blue sky, and in the mind of man,
A motion and a spirit, that impels
All thinking things, all objects of all thought,
And rolls through all things. Therefore am I still
A lover of the meadows and the woods,
And mountains; and of all that we behold
From this green earth; of all the mighty world
Of eye and ear, both what they half-create,
And what perceive; well pleased to recognize
In nature and the language of the sense,
The anchor of my purest thoughts, the nurse,
The guide, the guardian of my heart, and soul
Of all my moral being.

                Nor, perchance,
If I were not thus taught, should I the more
Suffer my genial spirits to decay:
For thou art with me, here, upon the banks
Of this fair river; thou, my dearest Friend,

My dear, dear Friend, and in thy voice I catch
The language of my former heart, and read
My former pleasures in the shooting lights
Of thy wild eyes. Oh! yet a little while
May I behold in thee what I was once,
My dear, dear Sister! And this prayer I make,
Knowing that Nature never did betray
The heart that loved her; 'tis her privilege,
Through all the years of this our life, to lead
From joy to joy: for she can so inform
The mind that is within us, so impress
With quietness and beauty, and so feed
With lofty thoughts, that neither evil tongues,
Rash judgments, nor the sneers of selfish men,
Nor greetings where no kindness is, nor all
The dreary intercourse of daily life,
Shall e'er prevail against us, or disturb
Our chearful faith that all which we behold
Is full of blessings. Therefore let the moon
Shine on thee in thy solitary walk;
And let the misty mountain winds be free
To blow against thee: and in after years,
When these wild ecstasies shall be matured

1798

Into a sober pleasure, when thy mind
Shall be a mansion for all lovely forms,
Thy memory be as a dwelling-place
For all sweet sounds and harmonies; Oh! then,
If solitude, or fear, or pain, or grief,
Should be thy portion, with what healing thoughts
Of tender joy wilt thou remember me,
And these my exhortations! Nor, perchance,
If I should be, where I no more can hear
Thy voice, nor catch from thy wild eyes these gleams
Of past existence, wilt thou then forget
That on the banks of this delightful stream
We stood together; and that I, so long
A worshipper of Nature, hither came
Unwearied in that service: rather say
With warmer love, oh! with far deeper zeal
Of holier love. Nor wilt thou then forget,
That after many wanderings, many years
Of absence, these steep woods and lofty cliffs,
And this green pastoral landscape, were to me
More dear, both for themselves, and for thy sake.

FROST AT MIDNIGHT

Samuel Taylor Coleridge

The Frost performs its secret ministry,
Unhelped by any wind. The owlet's cry
Came loud—and hark, again! loud as before.
The inmates of my cottage, all at rest,
Have left me to that solitude, which suits
Abstruser musings: save that at my side
My cradled infant slumbers peacefully.
'Tis calm indeed! so calm, that it disturbs
And vexes meditation with its strange
And extreme silentness. Sea, hill, and wood,
This populous village! Sea, and hill, and wood,
With all the numberless goings on of life,
Inaudible as dreams! the thin blue flame
Lies on my low burnt fire, and quivers not:
Only that film, which fluttered on the grate,
Still flutters there, the sole unquiet thing.
Methinks, its motion in this hush of nature
Gives it dim sympathies with me who live,
Making it a companionable form,   1798
Whose puny flaps and freaks the idling Spirit
By its own moods interprets, every where
Echo or mirror seeking of itself,
And makes a toy of Thought.

                              But O! how oft,
    How oft, at school, with most believing mind,
Presageful, have I gazed upon the bars,
To watch that fluttering *stranger*!⁷ and as oft
With unclosed lids, already had I dreamt
Of my sweet birth-place, and the old church-tower,
Whose bells, the poor man's only music, rang
From morn to evening, all the hot Fair-day,
So sweetly, that they stirred and haunted me
With a wild pleasure, falling on mine ear
Most like articulate sounds of things to come!
So gazed I, till the soothing things, I dreamt,

---

7 A stranger is a piece of soot. "In all parts of the kingdom these films are called strangers and supposed to portend the arrival of some absent friend" (Coleridge's note, 1798).

Lulled me to sleep, and sleep prolonged my dreams!
And so I brooded all the following morn,
Awed by the stern preceptor's face, mine eye
Fixed with mock study on my swimming book:
Save if the door half opened, and I snatched
A hasty glance, and still my heart leaped up,
For still I hoped to see the *stranger*'s face,
Townsman, or aunt, or sister more beloved,
My play-mate when we both were clothed alike!

Dear Babe, that sleepest cradled by my side,
Whose gentle breathings, heard in this deep calm,
Fill up the intersperséd vacancies
And momentary pauses of the thought!
My babe so beautiful! it thrills my heart
With tender gladness, thus to look at thee,
And think that thou shalt learn far other lore,
And in far other scenes! For I was reared
In the great city, pent 'mid cloisters dim,
And saw nought lovely but the sky and stars.
But *thou*, my babe! shalt wander like a breeze
By lakes and sandy shores, beneath the crags
Of ancient mountain, and beneath the clouds,
Which image in their bulk both lakes and shores
And mountain crags: so shalt thou see and hear
The lovely shapes and sounds intelligible
Of that eternal language, which thy God
Utters, who from eternity doth teach
Himself in all, and all things in himself.
Great universal Teacher! he shall mould
Thy spirit, and by giving make it ask.

Therefore all seasons shall be sweet to thee,
Whether the summer clothe the general earth
With greenness, or the redbreast sit and sing
Betwixt the tufts of snow on the bare branch
Of mossy apple-tree, while the night thatch
Smokes in the sun-thaw; whether the eve-drops fall
Heard only in the trances of the blast,
Or if the secret ministry of frost
Shall hang them up in silent icicles,
Quietly shining to the quiet Moon.

1798

THE RIME OF THE ANCYENT MARINERE

Samuel Taylor Coleridge

PART I

It is an ancyent Marinere,
  And he stoppeth one of three:
"By thy long grey beard and thy glittering eye
  Now wherefore stoppest thou me?

The Bridegroom's doors are open'd wide,
  And I am next of kin;
The Guests are met, the Feast is set,—
  May'st hear the merry din."

But still he holds the wedding-guest—
  There was a Ship, quoth he—
"Nay, if thou'st got a laughsome tale,
  Marinere! come with me."

He holds him with his skinny hand,
  Quoth he, there was a Ship—
"Now get thee hence, thou grey-beard Loon!
  Or my staff shall make thee skip."

1798

He holds him with his glittering eye—
  The wedding-guest stood still
And listens like a three year's child;
  The Marinere hath his will.

The wedding-guest sate on a stone,
  He cannot chuse but hear:
And thus spake on that ancyent man,
  The bright-eyed Marinere.

"The Ship was cheer'd, the Harbour clear'd—
  Merrily did we drop
Below the Kirk, below the Hill,
  Below the Light-house top.

The Sun came up upon the left,
  Out of the Sea came he:
And he shone bright, and on the right
  Went down into the Sea.

Higher and higher every day,
    Till over the mast at noon—"
The wedding-guest here beat his breast,
    For he heard the loud bassoon.

The Bride hath pac'd into the Hall,
    Red as a rose is she;
Nodding their heads before her goes
    The merry Minstralsy.

The wedding-guest he beat his breast,
    Yet he cannot chuse but hear:
And thus spake on that ancient Man,
    The bright-eyed Marinere.

"Listen, Stranger! Storm and Wind,
    A Wind and Tempest Strong!
For days and weeks it play'd us freaks—
    Life Chaff we drove along.

Listen, Stranger! Mist and Snow,
    And it grew wond'rous cauld:
And Ice mast-high came floating by
    As green as Emerauld.

And thro' the drifts the snowy clifts
    Did send a dismal sheen;
Ne shapes of men ne beasts we ken—
    The Ice was all between.

The Ice was here, the Ice was there,
    The Ice was all around:
It crack'd and growl'd, and roar'd and howl'd—
    Like noises of a swound.

At length did cross an Albatross,
    Through the Fog it came;
And an it were a Christian Soul,
    We hail'd it in God's name.

The Marineres gave it biscuit-worms,
    And round and round it flew:
The Ice did split with a Thunder-fit;
    The helmsman steer'd us thro'.

1798

56

And a good south wind sprung up behind,
    The Albatross did follow;
And every day, for food or play,
    Came to the Marinere's hollo!

In mist or cloud, on mast or shroud,
    It perch'd for vespers nine,
Whiles all the night, thro' fog-smoke white,
    Glimmer'd the white moon-shine.

"God save thee, ancyent Marinere!
    From the fiends that plague thee thus!—
Why look'st thou so?"—"With my cross bow
I shot the Albatross."

PART II

The Sun now rose upon the right;
    Out of the Sea came he;
And broad as a weft upon the left
    Went down into the Sea.

And the good south wind still blew behind,
    But no sweet Bird did follow
Ne any day for food or play
    Came to the Marinere's hollo!

And I had done an hellish thing
    And it would work 'em woe:
For all averr'd, I had kill'd the Bird
    That made the Breeze to blow.

Ne dim ne red, like God's own head,
    The glorious Sun uprist;
Then all averr'd, I had killed the Bird
    That brought the fog and mist.
'Twas right, said they, such birds to slay
    That bring the fog and mist.

The breezes blew, the white foam flew,
    The furrow follow'd free:
We were the first that ever burst
    Into that silent Sea.

1798

57

Down dropt the breeze, the Sails dropt down,
   'Twas sad as sad could be
And we did speak only to break
   The silence of the Sea.

All in a hot and copper sky
   The bloody Sun at noon,
Right up above the mast did stand,
   No bigger than the moon.

Day after day, day after day,
   We stuck, ne breath ne motion,
As idle as a painted Ship
   Upon a painted Ocean.

Water, water, every where,
   And all the boards did shrink;
Water, water, every where,
   Ne any drop to drink.

The very deeps did rot: O Christ!
   That ever this should be!
Yea, slimy things did crawl with legs
   Upon the slimy Sea.

1798

About, about, in reel and rout,
   The Death-fires danc'd at night;
The water, like a witch's oils,
   Burnt green and blue and white.

And some in dreams assurèd were
   Of the Spirit that plagued us so:
Nine fathom deep he had follow'd us
   From the Land of Mist and Snow.

And every tongue thro' utter drouth
   Was wither'd at the root;
We could not speak no more than if
   We had been choked with soot.

Ah wel-a-day! what evil looks
   Had I from old and young;
Instead of the Cross the Albatross
   About my neck was hung.

PART III

I saw a something in the Sky
  No bigger than my fist;
At first it seem'd a little speck
  And then it seem'd a mist:
It mov'd and mov'd, and took at last
  A certain shape, I wist.

A speck, a mist, a shape, I wist!
  And still it ner'd and ner'd;
As if it dodg'd a water-sprite,
  It plung'd and tack'd and veer'd.

With throat unslack'd, with black lips bak'd
  Ne could we laugh, ne wail:
Then while thro' drouth all dumb they stood
I bit my arm and suck'd the blood
  And cry'd, A sail! a sail!

With throat unslack'd, with black lips bak'd,
  Agape they hear'd me call;
Gramercy! they for joy did grin
And all at once their breath drew in
  As they were drinking all.

1798

She doth not tack from side to side—
  Hither to work us weal
Withouten wind, withouten tide
  She steddies with upright keel.

The western wave was all a flame,
  The day was well nigh done!
Almost upon the western wave
  Rested the broad bright Sun;
When that strange shape drove suddenly
  Betwixt us and the Sun.

And strait the Sun was fleck'd with bars
  (Heaven's mother send us grace)
As if thro' a dungeon grate he peer'd
  With broad and burning face.

Alas! (thought I, and my heart beat loud)
  How fast she neres and neres!
Are those *her* Sails that glance in the Sun
  Like restless gossameres?

59

Are those *her* naked ribs, which fleck'd
    The sun that did behind them peer?
And are those two all, all the crew,
    That woman and her fleshless Pheere?

His bones were black with many a crack,
    All black and bare, I ween;
Jet-black and bare, save where with rust
Of mouldy damps and charnel crust
    They're patch'd with purple and green.

Her lips are red, *her* looks are free,
    Her locks are yellow as gold:
Her skin is as white as leprosy,
And she is far liker Death than he;
    Her flesh makes the still air cold.

The naked Hulk alongside came
    And the Twain were playing dice;
"The Game is done! I've won, I've won!"
    Quoth she, and whistled thrice.

A gust of wind sterte up behind
    And whistled thro' his bones;
Thro' the holes of his eyes and the hole of his mouth
    Half-whistles and half-groans.

With never a whisper in the Sea
    Off darts the Spectre-ship;
While clombe above the Eastern bar
The horned Moon, with one bright Star
    Almost atween the tips.

One after one, by the horned Moon,
    (Listen, O Stranger! to me)
Each turn'd his face with a ghastly pang
    And curs'd me with his ee.

Four times fifty living men,
    With never a sigh or groan,
With heavy thump, a lifeless lump,
    They dropp'd down one by one.

Their souls did from their bodies fly,—
    They fled to bliss or woe;
And every soul it pass'd me by,
    Like the whiz of my Cross-bow.

1798

60

PART IV

"I fear thee, ancyent Marinere!
   I fear thy skinny hand;
And thou art long and lank and brown
   As is the ribb'd Sea-sand.

I fear thee and thy glittering eye
   And thy skinny hand so brown."—
"Fear not, fear not, thou wedding-guest!
   This body dropt not down.

Alone, alone, all all alone,
   Alone on the wide wide Sea;
And Christ would take no pity on
   My soul in agony.

The many men so beautiful,
   And they all dead did lie!
And a million million slimy things
   Liv'd on—and so did I.

I look'd upon the rotting Sea,
   And drew my eyes away;
I look'd upon the eldritch deck,
   And there the dead men lay.

I look'd to Heaven, and try'd to pray;
   But or ever a prayer had gusht,
A wicked whisper came and made
   My heart as dry as dust.

I clos'd my lids and kept them close,
   Till the balls like pulses beat;
For the sky and the sea, and the sea and the sky
Lay like a load on my weary eye,
   And the dead were at my feet.

The cold sweat melted from their limbs,
   Ne rot, ne reek did they;
The look with which they look'd on me,
   Had never pass'd away.

An orphan's curse would drag to Hell
   A spirit from on high:
But O! more horrible than that
   Is the curse in a dead man's eye!
Seven days, seven nights I saw that curse,
   And yet I could not die.

1798

61

The moving Moon went up the sky,
   And no where did abide:
Softly she was going up
   And a star or two beside—

Her beams bemock'd the sultry main
   Like morning frosts yspread;
But where the ship's huge shadow lay,
The charmèd water burnt alway
   A still and awful red.

Beyond the shadow of the ship
   I watch'd the water-snakes:
They mov'd in tracks of shining white;
And when they rear'd, the elfish light
   Fell off in hoary flakes.

Within the shadow of the ship
   I watch'd their rich attire:
Blue, glossy green, and velvet black
They coil'd and swam; and every track
   Was a flash of golden fire.

O happy living things! no tongue
   Their beauty might declare:
A spring of love gusht from my heart,
   And I bless'd them unaware!
Sure my kind saint took pity on me,
   And I bless'd them unaware.

1798

The self-same moment I could pray;
   And from my neck so free
The Albatross fell off, and sank
   Like lead into the sea.

PART V

O sleep! it is a gentle thing,
   Belov'd from pole to pole!
To Mary-queen the praise be yeven
She sent the gentle sleep from heaven
   That slid into my soul.

The silly buckets on the deck
   That had so long remain'd,
I dreamt that they were fill'd with dew
   And when I awoke, it rain'd.

My lips were wet, my throat was cold,
    My garments all were dank;
Sure I had drunken in my dreams,
    And still my body drank.

I mov'd and could not feel my limbs,
    I was so light, almost
I thought that I had died in sleep,
    And was a blessèd Ghost.

The roaring wind! it roar'd far off,
    It did not come anear;
But with its sound it shook the sails
    That were so thin and sere.

The upper air bursts into life,
    And a hundred fire-flags sheen,
To and fro they are hurried about;
And to and fro, and in and out
    The stars dance on between.

The coming wind doth roar more loud;
    The sails did sigh, like sedge:
The rain pours down from one black cloud;
    And the Moon is at its edge.

1798

Hark! hark! the thick black cloud is cleft,
    And the Moon is at its side:
Like waters shot from some high crag,
The lightning falls with never a jag
    A river steep and wide.

The strong wind reach'd the ship: it roar'd
    And dropp'd down, like a stone!
Beneath the lightning and the moon
    The dead men gave a groan.

They groan'd, they stirr'd, they all uprose,
    Ne spake, ne mov'd their eyes:
It had been strange, even in a dream
    To have seen those dead men rise.

The helmsman steerd, the ship mov'd on;
    Yet never a breeze up-blew;
The Marineres all 'gan work the ropes,
    Where they were wont to do:
They rais'd their limbs like lifeless tools—
    We were a ghastly crew.

The body of my brother's son
　　Stood by me knee to knee:
The body and I pull'd at one rope,
　　But he said nought to me—
And I quak'd to think of my own voice
　　How frightful it would be!

The day-light dawn'd—they dropp'd their arms,
　　And cluster'd round the mast:
Sweet sounds rose slowly thro' their mouths
　　And from their bodies pass'd.

Around, around, flew each sweet sound,
　　Then darted to the sun:
Slowly the sounds came back again
　　Now mix'd, now one by one.

Sometimes a-dropping from the sky,
　　I heard the Lavrock sing;
Sometimes all little birds that are
How they seem'd to fill the sea and air
　　With their sweet jargoning.

And now 'twas like all instruments,
　　Now like a lonely flute;
And now it is an angel's song,
　　That makes the heavens be mute.

1798

It ceas'd: yet still the sails made on
　　A pleasant noise till noon,
A noise like of a hidden brook
　　In the leafy month of June,
That to the sleeping woods all night
　　Singeth a quiet tune.

Listen, O listen, thou Wedding-guest!
　　"Marinere! thou hast thy will:
For that, which comes out of thine eye, doth make
　　My body and soul to be still"

Never sadder tale was told
　　To a man of woman born:
Sadder and wiser thou wedding-guest!
　　Thou'lt rise to morrow morn.

Never sadder tale was heard
　　By a man of woman born:
The Marineres all return'd to work
　　As silent as beforne.

The Marineres all 'gan pull the ropes,
  But look at me they n'old:
Thought I, I am as thin as air—
  They cannot me behold.

Till noon we silently sail'd on
  Yet never a breeze did breathe:
Slowly and smoothly went the ship
  Mov'd onward from beneath.

Under the keel nine fathom deep
  From the land of mist and snow
The spirit slid: and it was He
  That made the Ship to go.
The sails at noon left off their tune
  And the Ship stood still also.

The sun right up above the mast
  Had fix'd her to the ocean:
But in a minute she 'gan stir
  With a short uneasy motion—
Backwards and forwards half her length
  With a short uneasy motion.

Then, like a pawing horse let go,
  She made a sudden bound:
It flung the blood into my head,
  And I fell into a swound.

1798

How long in that same fit I lay,
  I have not to declare;
But ere my living life return'd,
I heard and in my soul discern'd
  Two voices in the air.

"Is it he?" quoth one, "Is this the man?
  By him who died on cross,
With his cruel bow he lay'd full low
  The harmless Albatross.

The spirit who 'bideth by himself
  In the land of mist and snow,
He lov'd the bird that lov'd the man
  Who shot him with his bow."

The other was a softer voice,
  As soft as honey-dew:
Quoth he, "The man hath penance done,
  And penance more will do."

PART VI

FIRST VOICE
"But tell me, tell me! speak again,
    Thy soft response renewing—
What makes that ship drive on so fast?
    What is the Ocean doing?"

SECOND VOICE
"Still as a Slave before his Lord,
    The Ocean hath no blast:
His great bright eye most silently
    Up to the moon is cast—

If he may know which way to go,
    For she guides him smooth or grim.
See, brother, see! how graciously
    She looketh down on him."

FIRST VOICE
"But why drives on that ship so fast
    Withouten wave or wind?"
SECOND VOICE
1798   "The air is cut away before,
    And closes from behind.

Fly, brother, fly! more high, more high!
    Or we shall be belated:
For slow and slow that ship will go,
    When the Marinere's trance is abated."

I woke, and we were sailing on
    As in a gentle weather:
'Twas night, calm night, the moon was high;
    The dead men stood together.

All stood together on the deck,
    For a charnel-dungeon fitter:
All fix'd on me their stony eyes
    That in the moon did glitter.

The pang, the curse, with which they died,
    Had never pass'd away:
I could not draw my een from theirs
    Ne turn them up to pray.

66

And in its time the spell was snapt,
    And I could move my een:
I look'd far-forth, but little saw
    Of what might else be seen.

Like one, that on a lonely road
    Doth walk in fear and dread,
And having once turn'd round, walks on
    And turns no more his head:
Because he knows, a frightful fiend
    Doth close behind him tread.

But soon there breath'd a wind on me,
    Ne sound ne motion made:
Its path was not upon the sea,
    In ripple or in shade.

It rais'd my hair, it fann'd my cheek,
    Like a meadow-gale of spring—
It mingled strangely with my fears,
    Yet it felt like a welcoming.

Swiftly, swiftly flew the ship,
    Yet she sail'd softly too:
Sweetly, sweetly blew the breeze—
    On me alone it blew.

O dream of joy! is this indeed
    The light-house top I see?
Is this the Hill? Is this the Kirk?
    Is this mine own countree?

We drifted o'er the Harbour-bar,
    And I with sobs did pray—
"O let me be awake, my God!
    Or let me sleep alway!"

The harbour-bay was clear as glass,
    So smoothly it was strewn!
And on the bay the moon light lay,
    And the shadow of the moon.

The moonlight bay was white all o'er,
    Till rising from the same,
Full many shapes, that shadows were,
    Like as of torches came.

1798

A little distance from the prow
    Those dark-red shadows were;
But soon I saw that my own flesh
    Was red as in a glare.

I turn'd my head in fear and dread,
    And by the holy rood,
The bodies had advanc'd, and now
    Before the mast they stood.

They lifted up their stiff right arms,
    They held them strait and tight;
And each right-arm burnt like a torch,
    A torch that's borne upright.
Their stony eye-balls glitter'd on
    In the red and smoky light.

I pray'd and turn'd my head away
    Forth looking as before.
There was no breeze upon the bay,
    No wave against the shore.

The rock shone bright, the kirk no less
    That stands above the rock:
The moonlight steep'd in silentness
    The steady weathercock.

1798

And the bay was white with silent light,
    Till rising from the same
Full many shapes, that shadows were,
    In crimson colours came.

A little distance from the prow
    Those crimson shadows were:
I turn'd my eyes upon the deck—
    O Christ! what saw I there?

Each corse lay flat, lifeless and flat;
    And by the Holy rood,
A man all light, a seraph-man,
    On every corse there stood.

This seraph-band, each wav'd his hand:
    It was a heavenly sight:
They stood as signals to the land,
    Each one a lovely light:

This seraph-band, each wav'd his hand,
    No voice did they impart—
No voice; but O! the silence sank,
    Like music on my heart.

Eftsones I heard the dash of oars,
    I heard the pilot's cheer:
My head was turn'd perforce away,
    And I saw a boat appear.

Then vanish'd all the lovely lights;
    The bodies rose anew:
With silent pace, each to his place,
    Came back the ghastly crew.
The wind, that shade nor motion made,
    On me alone it blew.

The pilot, and the pilot's boy
    I heard them coming fast:
Dear Lord in Heaven! it was a joy,
    The dead men could not blast.

I saw a third—I heard his voice:
    It is the Hermit good!
He singeth loud his godly hymns
    That he makes in the wood.
He'll shrieve my soul, he'll wash away
    The Albatross's blood.

1798

PART VII

This Hermit good lives in that wood
    Which slopes down to the Sea.
How loudly his sweet voice he rears!
He loves to talk with Marineres
    That come from a far Countree.

He kneels at morn and noon and eve—
    He hath a cushion plump:
It is the moss, that wholly hides
    The rotted old Oak-stump.

The Skiff-boat ne'rd: I heard them talk,
    "Why, this is strange, I trow!
Where are those lights so many and fair
    That signal made but now?"

"Strange, by my faith!" the Hermit said—
    "And they answer'd not our cheer.
The planks look warp'd, and see those sails
    How thin they are and sere!
I never saw aught like to them
    Unless perchance it were

The skeletons of leaves that lag
    My forest-brook along:
When the Ivy-tod is heavy with snow,
And the Owlet whoops to the wolf below
    That eats the she-wolf's young."

"Dear Lord! it has a fiendish look—
    (The Pilot made reply)
"I am afear'd."—"Push on, push on!"
    Said the Hermit cheerily.

The Boat came closer to the Ship,
    But I ne spake ne stirr'd!
The Boat came close beneath the Ship,
    And strait a sound was heard!

1798

Under the water it rumbled on,
    Still louder and more dread:
It reach'd the Ship, it split the bay;
    The Ship went down like lead.

Stunn'd by that loud and dreadful sound,
    Which sky and ocean smote:
Like one that hath been seven days drown'd
    My body lay afloat:
But, swift as dreams, myself I found
    Within the Pilot's boat.

Upon the whirl, where sank the Ship,
    The boat spun round and round:
And all was still, save that the hill
    Was telling of the sound.

I mov'd my lips: the Pilot shriek'd
    And fell down in a fit.
The Holy Hermit rais'd his eyes
    And pray'd where he did sit.

I took the oars: the Pilot's boy,
    Who now doth crazy go,
Laugh'd loud and long, and all the while
    His eyes went to and fro.
"Ha! ha!" quoth he—"full plain I see,
    The devil knows how to row."

And now all in mine own Countree
    I stood on the firm land!
The Hermit stepp'd forth from the boat,
    And scarcely he could stand.

"O shrieve me, shrieve me, holy Man!"
    The Hermit cross'd his brow—
"Say quick," quoth he, "I bid thee say
    What manner man art thou?"

Forthwith this frame of mine was wrench'd
    With a woeful agony,
Which forc'd me to begin my tale
    And then it left me free.

Since then at an uncertain hour,
    Now oftimes and now fewer,
That anguish comes and makes me tell
    My ghastly aventure.

I pass, like night, from land to land;
    I have strange power of speech;
The moment that his face I see
I know the man that must hear me;
    To him my tale I teach.

What loud uproar bursts from that door!
    The Wedding-guests are there;
But in the Garden-bower the Bride
    And Bride-maids singing are:
And hark the little Vesper-bell
    Which biddeth me to prayer.

O Wedding-guest! this soul hath been
    Alone on a wide wide sea:
So lonely 'twas, that God himself
    Scarce seemed there to be.

1798

71

O sweeter than the Marriage-feast,
   'Tis sweeter far to me
To walk together to the Kirk
   With a goodly company.

To walk together to the Kirk
   And all together pray,
While each to his great father bends,
Old men, and babes, and loving friends,
   And Youths, and Maidens gay.

Farewell, farewell! but this I tell
   To thee, thou wedding-guest!
He prayeth well who loveth well,
   Both man and bird and beast.

He prayeth best who loveth best,
   All things both great and small:
For the dear God, who loveth thus,
   He made and loveth all.

The Marinere, whose eye is bright,
   Whose beard with age is hoar,
Is gone; and now the wedding-guest
   Turn'd from the bridegroom's door.

He went, like one that hath been stunn'd
   And is of sense forlorn:
A sadder and a wiser man
   He rose the morrow morn.

1798

FRANCE: AN ODE

Samuel Taylor Coleridge

I.

Ye Clouds! that far above me float and pause,
   Whose pathless march no mortal may controul!
   Ye Ocean-Waves! that, wheresoe'er ye roll,
Yield homage only to eternal laws!
Ye Woods! that listen to the night-birds' singing,
   Midway the smooth and perilous slope reclined,
Save when your own imperious branches swinging,
   Have made a solemn music of the wind!

Where, like a man beloved of God,
Through glooms, which never woodman trod,
   How oft, pursuing fancies holy,
My moonlight way o'er flowering weeds I wound,
   Inspired, beyond the guess of folly,
By each rude shape and wild unconquerable sound!
O ye loud Waves! and O ye Forests high!
  And O ye Clouds that far above me soared!
Thou rising Sun! thou blue rejoicing Sky!
  Yea, every thing that is and will be free!
Bear witness for me, wheresoe'er ye be,
With what deep worship I have still adored
   The spirit of divinest Liberty.

II.

When France in wrath her giant-limbs upreared,
   And with that oath, which smote air, earth, and sea,
   Stamped her strong foot and said she would be free,
Bear witness for me, how I hoped and feared!
With what a joy my lofty gratulation
   Unawed I sang, amid a slavish band:
And when to whelm the disenchanted nation,
   Like fiends embattled by a wizard's wand,
    The Monarchs marched in evil day,
    And Britain joined the dire array;
   Though dear her shores and circling ocean,
Though many friendships, many youthful loves
   Had swoln the patriot emotion
And flung a magic light o'er all her hills and groves;
Yet still my voice, unaltered, sang defeat
   To all that braved the tyrant-quelling lance,
And shame too long delayed and vain retreat!
For ne'er, O Liberty! with partial aim
I dimmed thy light or damped thy holy flame;
   But blessed the paeans of delivered France,
And hung my head and wept at Britain's name.

1798

III.

"And what," I said, "though Blasphemy's loud scream
   With that sweet music of deliverance strove!
   Though all the fierce and drunken passions wove
A dance more wild than e'er was maniac's dream!
   Ye storms, that round the dawning East assembled,
The Sun was rising, though he hid his light!"
And when, to soothe my soul, that hoped and trembled,
The dissonance ceased, and all seemed calm and bright;

When France her front deep-scarr'd and gory
Concealed with clustering wreaths of glory;
    When, insupportably advancing,
Her arm made mockery of the warrior's tramp;
    While timid looks of fury glancing,
Domestic treason, crushed beneath her fatal stamp,
Writhed like a wounded dragon in his gore;
    Then I reproached my fears that would not flee;
"And soon," I said, "shall Wisdom teach her lore
In the low huts of them that toil and groan!
And, conquering by her happiness alone,
    Shall France compel the nations to be free,
Till Love and Joy look round, and call the Earth their own."

IV.

Forgive me, Freedom! O forgive those dreams!
    I hear thy voice, I hear thy loud lament,
    From bleak Helvetia's icy caverns sent—
I hear thy groans upon her blood-stained streams!
    Heroes, that for your peaceful country perished,
And ye that, fleeing, spot your mountain-snows
    With bleeding wounds; forgive me, that I cherished
One thought that ever blessed your cruel foes!
    To scatter rage, and traitorous guilt,
    Where Peace her jealous home had built;
        A patriot-race to disinherit
Of all that made their stormy wilds so dear;
    And with inexpiable spirit
To taint the bloodless freedom of the mountaineer—
O France, that mockest Heaven, adulterous, blind,
    And patriot only in pernicious toils!
Are these thy boasts, Champion of human kind?
    To mix with Kings in the low lust of sway,
Yell in the hunt, and share the murderous prey;
To insult the shrine of Liberty with spoils
    From freemen torn; to tempt and to betray?

V.

The Sensual and the Dark rebel in vain,
    Slaves by their own compulsion! In mad game
    They burst their manacles and wear the name
        Of Freedom, graven on a heavier chain!
        O Liberty! with profitless endeavour
Have I pursued thee, many a weary hour;
    But thou nor swell'st the victor's strain, nor ever
Didst breathe thy soul in forms of human power.

1798

Alike from all, howe'er they praise thee,
  (Nor prayer, nor boastful name delays thee)
    Alike from Priestcraft's harpy minions,
  And factious Blasphemy's obscener slaves,
    Thou speedest on thy subtle pinions,
The guide of homeless winds, and playmate of the waves!
And there I felt thee!—on that sea-cliff's verge,
  Whose pines, scarce travelled by the breeze above,
Had made one murmur with the distant surge!
Yes, while I stood and gazed, my temples bare,
And shot my being through earth, sea, and air,
  Possessing all things with intensest love,
    O Liberty! my spirit felt thee there.

THE BALLAD OF THE DARK LADIE

Samuel Taylor Coleridge

Beneath yon birch with silver bark,
And boughs so pendulous and fair,
The brook falls scatter'd down the rock:
    And all is mossy there!

And there upon the moss she sits,
The Dark Ladie in silent pain;
The heavy tear is in her eye,
    And drops and swells again.

Three times she sends her little page
Up the castled mountain's breast,
If he might find the Knight that wears
    The Griffin for his crest.

The sun was sloping down the sky,
And she had linger'd there all day,
Counting moments, dreaming fears—
    O wherefore can he stay?

She hears a rustling o'er the brook,
She sees far off a swinging bough!
"'Tis He! 'Tis my betrothed Knight!
    Lord Falkland, it is Thou!"

She springs, she clasps him round the neck,
She sobs a thousand hopes and fears,
Her kisses glowing on his cheeks
    She quenches with her tears.

1798

* * * * *

"My friends with rude ungentle words
They scoff and bid me fly to thee!
O give me shelter in thy breast!
    O shield and shelter me!

"My Henry, I have given thee much,
I gave what I can ne'er recall,
I gave my heart, I gave my peace,
    O Heaven! I gave thee all."

The Knight made answer to the Maid,
While to his heart he held her hand,
"Nine castles hath my noble sire,
    None statelier in the land.

"The fairest one shall be my love's,
The fairest castle of the nine!
Wait only till the stars peep out,
    The fairest shall be thine:

"Wait only till the hand of eve
Hath wholly closed yon western bars,
And through the dark we two will steal
    Beneath the twinkling stars!"—

"The dark? the dark? No! not the dark?
The twinkling stars? How, Henry? How?
O God! 'twas in the eye of noon
    He pledged his sacred vow!

"And in the eye of noon my love
Shall lead me from my mother's door,
Sweet boys and girls all clothed in white
    Strewing flowers before:

"But first the nodding minstrels go
With music meet for lordly bowers,
The children next in snow-white vests,
    Strewing buds and flowers!

"And then my love and I shall pace,
My jet black hair in pearly braids,
Between our comely bachelors
    And blushing bridal maids."

* * * * *

1798

SONG
(SHE DWELT AMONG TH' UNTRODDEN WAYS)
William Wordsworth

She dwelt among th' untrodden ways
   Beside the springs of Dove,
A Maid whom there were none to praise
   And very few to love.

A Violet by a mossy stone
   Half-hidden from the Eye!
—Fair, as a star when only one
   Is shining in the sky!

She *liv'd* unknown, and few could know
   When Lucy ceas'd to be;
But she is in her Grave, and Oh!
   The difference to me.

LUCY GRAY
William Wordsworth

1798

Oft had I heard of Lucy Gray,
And when I cross'd the Wild,
I chanc'd to see at break of day
The solitary Child.

No Mate, no comrade Lucy knew;
She dwelt on a wide Moor,
The sweetest Thing that ever grew
Beside a human door!

You yet may spy the Fawn at play,
The Hare upon the Green;
But the sweet face of Lucy Gray
Will never more be seen.

"To-night will be a stormy night,
You to the Town must go,
And take a lantern, Child, to light
Your Mother thro' the snow."

"That, Father! will I gladly do;
'Tis scarcely afternoon—
The Minster-clock has just struck two,
And yonder is the Moon."

At this the Father rais'd his hook
And snapp'd a faggot-band;
He plied his work, and Lucy took
The lantern in her hand.

Not blither is the mountain roe,
With many a wanton stroke
Her feet disperse the powd'ry snow
That rises up like smoke.

The storm came on before its time,
She wander'd up and down,
And many a hill did Lucy climb
But never reach'd the Town.

The wretched Parents all that night
Went shouting far and wide;
But there was neither sound nor sight
To serve them for a guide.

At day-break on a hill they stood
That overlook'd the Moor;
And thence they saw the Bridge of Wood
A furlong from their door.

And now they homeward turn'd, and cry'd
"In Heaven we all shall meet!"
When in the snow the Mother spied
The print of Lucy's feet.

Then downward from the steep hill's edge
They track'd the footmarks small;
And through the broken hawthorn-hedge,
And by the long stone-wall;

And then an open field they cross'd,
The marks were still the same;
They track'd them on, nor ever lost,
And to the Bridge they came.

They follow'd from the snowy bank
The footmarks, one by one,
Into the middle of the plank,
And further there were none.

Yet some maintain that to this day
She is a living Child,
That you may see sweet Lucy Gray
Upon the lonesome Wild.

O'er rough and smooth she trips along,
And never looks behind;
And sings a solitary song
That whistles in the wind.

THE OLD FAMILIAR FACES

Charles Lamb

I have had playmates, I have had companions,
In my days of childhood, in my joyful school-days,
All, all are gone, the old familiar faces.

1798

I have been laughing, I have been carousing,
Drinking late, sitting late, with my bosom cronies,
All, all are gone, the old familiar faces.

I loved a love once, fairest among women;
Closed are her doors on me, I must not see her—
All, all are gone, the old familiar faces.

I have a friend, a kinder friend has no man;
Like an ingrate, I left my friend abruptly;
Left him, to muse on the old familiar faces.

Ghost-like I paced round the haunts of my childhood.
Earth seemed a desart I was bound to traverse,
Seeking to find the old familiar faces.

Friend of my bosom, thou more than a brother,
Why wert not thou born in my father's dwelling?
So might we talk of the old familiar faces—

How some they have died, and some they have left me,
And some are taken from me; all are departed;
All, all are gone, the old familiar faces.

COMPOSED AT MIDNIGHT

Charles Lamb

From broken visions of perturbed rest
I wake, and start, and fear to sleep again.
How total a privation of all sounds,
Sights, and familiar objects, man, bird, beast,
Herb, tree, or flower, and prodigal light of heaven.
'Twere some relief to catch the drowsy cry
Of the mechanic watchman, or the noise
Of revel reeling home from midnight cups.
Those are the moanings of the dying man,
Who lies in the upper chamber; restless moans,
And interrupted only by a cough
Consumptive, torturing the wasted lungs.
So in the bitterness of death he lies,
And waits in anguish for the morning's light.
What can that do for him, or what restore?
Short taste, faint sense, affecting notices,
And little images of pleasures past,
Of health, and active life—health not yet slain,
Nor the other grace of life, a good name, sold
For sin's black wages. On his tedious bed
He writhes, and turns him from the accusing light,
And finds no comfort in the sun, but says
"When night comes I shall get a little rest."
Some few groans more, death comes, and there an end.
'Tis darkness and conjecture all beyond;
Weak Nature fears, though Charity must hope,
And Fancy, most licentious on such themes
Where decent reverence well had kept her mute,
Hath o'er-stock'd hell with devils, and brought down
By her enormous fablings and mad lies,
Discredit on the gospel's serious truths
And salutary fears. The man of parts,
Poet, or prose declaimer, on his couch
Lolling, like one indifferent, fabricates
A heaven of gold, where he, and such as he,
Their heads encompassed with crowns, their heels
With fine wings garlanded, shall tread the stars

1798

80

Beneath their feet, heaven's pavement, far removed
From damnèd spirits, and the torturing cries
Of men, his breth'ren, fashioned of the earth,
As he was, nourish'd with the self-same bread,
Belike his kindred or companions once—
Through everlasting ages now divorced,
In chains and savage torments to repent
Short years of folly on earth. Their groans unheard
In heav'n, the saint nor pity feels, nor care,
For those thus sentenced—pity might disturb
The delicate sense and most divine repose
Of spirits angelical. Blessed be God,
The measure of his judgements is not fix'd
By man's erroneous standard. He discerns
No such inordinate difference and vast
Betwixt the sinner and the saint, to doom
Such disproportion'd fates. Compared with him,
No man on earth is holy call'd: they best
Stand in his sight approved, who at his feet
Their little crowns of virtue cast, and yield
To him of his own works the praise, his due.

1798

1799

TO A LITTLE INVISIBLE BEING
WHO IS EXPECTED SOON TO BECOME VISIBLE

Anna Letitia Barbauld

Germ of new life, whose powers expanding slow
For many a moon their full perfection wait,—
Haste, precious pledge of happy love, to go
Auspicious borne through life's mysterious gate.

What powers lie folded in thy curious frame,—
Senses from objects locked, and mind from thought!
How little canst thou guess thy lofty claim
To grasp at all the worlds the Almighty wrought!

And see, the genial season's warmth to share,
Fresh younglings shoot, and opening roses glow!
Swarms of new life exulting fill the air,—
Haste, infant bud of being, haste to blow!

For thee the nurse prepares her lulling songs,
The eager matrons count the lingering day;
But far the most thy anxious parent longs
On thy soft cheek a mother's kiss to lay.

She only asks to lay her burden down,
That her glad arms that burden may resume;
And nature's sharpest pangs her wishes crown,
That free thee living from thy living tomb.

She longs to fold to her maternal breast
Part of herself, yet to herself unknown;
To see and to salute the stranger guest,
Fed with her life through many a tedious moon.

Come, reap thy rich inheritance of love!
Bask in the fondness of a Mother's eye!
Nor wit nor eloquence her heart shall move
Like the first accents of thy feeble cry.

Haste, little captive, burst thy prison doors!
Launch on the living world, and spring to light!
Nature for thee displays her various stores,
Opens her thousand inlets of delight.

If charmed verse or muttered prayers had power,
With favouring spells to speed thee on thy way,
Anxious I'd bid my beads each passing hour,
Till thy wished smile thy mother's pangs o'erpay.

1800

THERE WAS A BOY
William Wordsworth

There was a Boy, ye knew him well, ye Cliffs
And Islands of Winander![8]—many a time,
At evening, when the earliest stars began
To move along the edges of the hills,
Rising or setting, would he stand alone,
Beneath the trees, or by the glimmering lake;
And there, with fingers interwoven, both hands
Pressed closely palm to palm and to his mouth
Uplifted, he, as through an instrument,
Blew mimic hootings to the silent owls,
That they might answer him.—And they would shout
Across the watery vale, and shout again
Responsive to his call,—with quivering peals,
And long halloos, and screams, and echoes loud
Redoubled and redoubled; concourse wild
Of mirth and jocund din! And, when it chanced
That pauses of deep silence mocked his skill,
Then, sometimes, in that silence, while he hung
Listening, a gentle shock of mild surprise
Has carried far into his heart the voice
Of mountain torrents; or the visible scene
Would enter unawares into his mind
With all its solemn imagery, its rocks,
Its woods, and that uncertain heaven, received
Into the bosom of the steady lake.

   This Boy was taken from his Mates, and died
In childhood, ere he was full twelve years old.
Fair is the spot, most beautiful the Vale
Where he was born: the grassy Church-yard hangs
Upon a slope above the village school;
And, through that Church-yeard when my way has led
At evening, I believe, that oftentimes
A long half-hour together I have stood
Mute—looking at the grave in which he lies!

8 Lake Windermere (formerly known as Winander Mere), the
largest natural lake in England, in the Lake District.

1800

THREE YEARS SHE GREW

William Wordsworth

Three years she grew in sun and shower,
Then Nature said, "A lovelier flower
On earth was never sown;
This Child I to myself will take,
She shall be mine, and I will make
A Lady of my own.

Myself will to my darling be
Both law and impulse, and with me
The Girl in rock and plain,
In earth and heaven, in glade and bower,
Shall feel an overseeing power
To kindle or restrain.

She shall be sportive as the fawn
That wild with glee across the lawn
Or up the mountain springs,
And hers shall be the breathing balm,
And hers the silence and the calm
Of mute insensate things.

The floating clouds their state shall lend
To her, for her the willow bend,
Nor shall she fail to see
Even in the motions of the storm
A beauty that shall mould her form
By silent sympathy.

1800

The stars of midnight shall be dear
To her, and she shall lean her ear
In many a secret place
Where rivulets dance their wayward round,
And beauty born of murmuring sound
Shall pass into her face.

And vital feelings of delight
Shall rear her form to stately height,
Her virgin bosom swell,
Such thoughts to Lucy I will give
While she and I together live
Here in this happy dell."

Thus Nature spake—The work was done—
How soon my Lucy's race was run!
She died and left to me
This heath, this calm and quiet scene,
The memory of what has been,
And never more will be.

84

1802

TO TOUSSAINT L'OUVERTURE
William Wordsworth

Toussaint, the most unhappy man of men!
Whether the whistling Rustic tend his plough
Within thy hearing, or thy head be now
Pillowed in some deep dungeon's earless den; —
O miserable Chieftain! Where and when
Wilt thou find patience? Yet die not: do thou
Wear rather in thy bonds a cheerful brow:
Though fallen thyself, never to rise again,
Live, and take comfort. Thou hast left behind
Powers that will work for thee; air, earth, and skies;
There's not a breathing of the common wind
That will forget thee; thou hast great allies;
Thy friends are exultations, agonies,
And love, and man's unconquerable mind.

NEAR DOVER, SEPTEMBER 1802
William Wordsworth

Inland, within a hollow vale I stood;
And saw, while sea was calm and air was clear,
The coast of France—the coast of France how near!
Drawn almost into frightful neighbourhood.
I shrunk; for verily the barrier flood
Was like a lake, or river bright and fair,
A span of waters; yet what power is there!
What mightiness for evil and for good!
Even so doth God protect us if we be
Virtuous and wise. Winds blow, and waters roll,
Strength to the brave, and Power, and Deity;
Yet in themselves are nothing! One decree
Spake laws to *them*, and said that by the soul
Only, the Nations shall be great and free.

COMPOSED UPON WESTMINSTER BRIDGE, SEPTEMBER 3 1802

William Wordsworth

Earth has not any thing to show more fair:
Dull would he be of soul who could pass by
A sight so touching in its majesty:
This City now doth, like a garment, wear
The beauty of the morning; silent, bare,
Ships, towers, domes, theatres, and temples lie
Open unto the fields, and to the sky;
All bright and glittering in the smokeless air.
Never did sun more beautifully steep
In his first splendour, valley, rock, or hill;
Ne'er saw I, never felt, a calm so deep!
The river glideth at his own sweet will:
Dear God! the very houses seem asleep;
And all that mighty heart is lying still!

LONDON, 1802

William Wordsworth

Milton! thou shouldst be living at this hour:
England hath need of thee: she is a fen
Of stagnant waters: altar, sword, and pen,
Fireside, the heroic wealth of hall and bower,
Have forfeited their ancient English dower
Of inward happiness. We are selfish men;
Oh! raise us up, return to us again;
And give us manners, virtue, freedom, power.
Thy soul was like a Star, and dwelt apart:
Thou hadst a voice whose sound was like the sea:
Pure as the naked heavens, majestic, free,
So didst thou travel on life's common way,
In cheerful godliness; and yet thy heart
The lowliest duties on herself did lay.

GREAT MEN HAVE BEEN AMONG US

William Wordsworth

Great men have been among us; hands that penned
And tongues that uttered wisdom—better none:
The later Sidney, Marvel, Harrington,
Young Vane, and others who called Milton friend.
These moralists could act and comprehend:
They knew how genuine glory was put on;
Taught us how rightfully a nation shone
In splendour: what strength was, that would not bend
But in magnanimous meekness. France, 'tis strange,
Hath brought forth no such souls as we had then.
Perpetual emptiness! unceasing change!
No single volume paramount, no code,
No master spirit, no determined road;
But equally a want of books and men!

TO AN OLD OAK   1802

Samuel Rogers

Immota manet; multosque nepotes,
Multa virum volvens durando sæcula, vincit.[9]
Virgil

Round thee, alas, no shadows move!
From thee no sacred murmurs breathe!
Yet within thee, thyself a grove,
Once did the eagle scream above,
And the wolf howl beneath.

There once the steel-clad knight reclin'd,
His sable plumage tempest-toss'd;
And, as the death-bell smote the wind,
From towers long fled by human kind,
His brow the hero cross'd.

---

9 Translated: "unmoved it abides; see children's children die
through long generation of men as the victor years roll by". From
Virgil's *Georgics II*, l. 294-295.

Then Culture came, and days serene;
And village-sports, and garlands gay.
Full many a pathway cross'd the green;
And maids and shepherd-youths were seen
To celebrate the May.

Father of many a forest deep,
Whence many a navy thunder-fraught;
Erst in their acorn-cells asleep,
Soon destin'd o'er the world to sweep,
Opening new spheres of thought!

Wont in the night of woods to dwell,
The holy druid saw thee rise;
And, planting there the guardian-spell,
Sung forth, the dreadful pomp to swell
Of human sacrifice!

Thy singed top and branches bare
Now straggle in the evening sky;
And the wan moon round to glare
On the long corse that shivers there
Of him who came to die!

1802

1803

TO THE FRAGMENT OF A STATUE OF HERCULES, COMMONLY CALLED THE TORSO
Samuel Rogers

And dost thou still, thou mass of breathing stone,
(Thy giant limbs to night and chaos hurl'd)
Still sit as on the fragment of a world;
Surviving all, majestic and alone?
What tho' the Spirits of the North, that swept
Rome from the earth, when in her pomp she slept,
Smote thee with fury, and thy headless trunk
Deep in the dust mid tower and temple sunk;
Soon to subdue mankind 'twas thine to rise,
Still, still unquell'd thy glorious energies!
Aspiring minds, with thee conversing, caught[10]
Bright revelations of the Good they sought;
By thee that long-lost spell[11] in secret giv'n,
To draw down Gods, and life the soul to Heav'n!

1803

---

10 Author's note: "In the gardens of the Vatican where it was placed by Julius II, it was long the favourite study of those great men, to whom we owe the revival of the arts, Michael Angelo, Raphael, and the Caracci."
11 Author's note: "Once in the possession of Praxiteles, if we may believe an antient epigram on the Gnidian Venus (*Analecta Vet. Poetarum*, III. 200)."

1804

MOCK ON, MOCK ON, VOLTAIRE, ROUSSEAU
William Blake

Mock on, Mock on, Voltaire, Rousseau;
   Mock on, mock on; 'tis all in vain!
You throw the sand against the wind,
   And the wind blows it back again.

And every sand becomes a Gem
   Reflected in the beams divine;
Blown back, they blind the mocking Eye,
   But still in Israel's paths they shine.

The Atoms of Democritus

   And Newton's Particles of light
Are sands upon the Red Sea shore,
   Where Israel's tents do shine so bright.

I WANDERED LONELY AS A CLOUD

1804

William Wordsworth

I wandered lonely as a cloud
That floats on high o'er vales and hills,
When all at once I saw a crowd,
A host, of golden daffodils;
Beside the lake, beneath the trees,
Fluttering and dancing in the breeze.

Continuous as the stars that shine
And twinkle on the milky way,
They stretched in never-ending line
Along the margin of a bay:
Ten thousand saw I at a glance,
Tossing their heads in sprightly dance.

The waves beside them danced; but they
Out-did the sparkling waves in glee:
A poet could not but be gay,
In such a jocund company:
I gazed—and gazed— but little thought
What wealth the show to me had brought:

For oft, when on my couch I lie
In vacant or in pensive mood,
They flash upon that inward eye
Which is the bliss of solitude;
And then my heart with pleasure fills,
And dances with the daffodils.

THE FRENCH REVOLUTION AS IT APPEARED TO ENTHUSIASTS AT ITS COMMENCEMENT
William Wordsworth

Oh! pleasant exercise of hope and joy!
For mighty were the auxiliars which then stood
Upon our side, we who were strong in love!
Bliss was it in that dawn to be alive,
But to be young was very heaven!—Oh! times,
In which the meagre, stale, forbidding ways
Of custom, law, and statute, took at once
The attraction of a country in romance!
When Reason seemed the most to assert her rights,
When most intent on making of herself
A prime Enchantress—to assist the work,   1804
Which then was going forward in her name!
Not favoured spots alone, but the whole earth,
The beauty wore of promise, that which sets
(As at some moment might not be unfelt
Among the bowers of paradise itself)
The budding rose above the rose full blown.
What temper at the prospect did not wake
To happiness unthought of? The inert
Were roused, and lively natures rapt away!
They who had fed their childhood upon dreams,
The playfellows of fancy, who had made
All powers of swiftness, subtilty, and strength
Their ministers,—who in lordly wise had stirred
Among the grandest objects of the sense,
And dealt with whatsoever they found there
As if they had within some lurking right
To wield it;—they, too, who, of gentle mood,
Had watched all gentle motions, and to these
Had fitted their own thoughts, schemers more mild,
And in the region of their peaceful selves;—

Now was it that both found, the meek and lofty
Did both find, helpers to their heart's desire,
And stuff at hand, plastic as they could wish;
Were called upon to exercise their skill,
Not in Utopia, subterranean fields,
Or some secreted island, Heaven knows where!
But in the very world, which is the world
Of all of us,—the place where in the end
We find our happiness, or not at all!

INTIMATIONS OF IMMORTALITY
FROM RECOLLECTIONS OF EARLY CHILDHOOD

William Wordsworth

The child is father of the man;
And I could wish my days to be
Bound each to each by natural piety.
(Wordsworth, "My heart leaps up")

1804

There was a time when meadow, grove, and stream,
The earth, and every common sight,
　　　To me did seem
　　　Apparelled in celestial light,
The glory and the freshness of a dream.
It is not now as it hath been of yore;—
　　　Turn wheresoe'er I may,
　　　　By night or day.
The things which I have seen I now can see no more.

　　　The Rainbow comes and goes,
　　　And lovely is the Rose,
　　　The Moon doth with delight
Look round her when the heavens are bare,
　　　Waters on a starry night
　　　Are beautiful and fair;
　　The sunshine is a glorious birth;
　　But yet I know, where'er I go,
That there hath past away a glory from the earth.

Now, while the birds thus sing a joyous song,
　　And while the young lambs bound
　　　As to the tabor's sound,
To me alone there came a thought of grief:

A timely utterance gave that thought relief,
　　　　And I again am strong:
The cataracts blow their trumpets from the steep;
No more shall grief of mine the season wrong;
I hear the Echoes through the mountains throng,
The Winds come to me from the fields of sleep,
　　　　And all the earth is gay;
　　　　Land and sea
　　Give themselves up to jollity,
　　　　And with the heart of May
　　Doth every Beast keep holiday;—
　　　　Thou Child of Joy,
Shout round me, let me hear thy shouts, thou happy
　　　　Shepherd-boy!

Ye blessèd creatures, I have heard the call
　　Ye to each other make; I see
The heavens laugh with you in your jubilee;
　　My heart is at your festival,
　　　　My head hath its coronal,
The fulness of your bliss, I feel—I feel it all.
　　　　Oh evil day! if I were sullen
　　　　While Earth herself is adorning,
　　　　　This sweet May-morning,
　　　　And the Children are culling
　　　　　On every side,
　　　　In a thousand valleys far and wide,
　　　　Fresh flowers; while the sun shines warm,
And the Babe leaps up on his Mother's arm:—
　　　　I hear, I hear, with joy I hear!
　　　　—But there's a Tree, of many, one,
A single Field which I have looked upon,
Both of them speak of something that is gone:
　　　　The Pansy at my feet
　　　　Doth the same tale repeat:
Whither is fled the visionary gleam?
Where is it now, the glory and the dream?

Our birth is but a sleep and a forgetting:
The Soul that rises with us, our life's Star,
　　　　Hath had elsewhere its setting,
　　　　And cometh from afar:
　　　　Not in entire forgetfulness,
　　　　And not in utter nakedness,
But trailing clouds of glory do we come
　　　　From God, who is our home:
Heaven lies about us in our infancy!
Shades of the prison-house begin to close

1804

93

Upon the growing Boy,
But he beholds the light, and whence it flows,
He sees it in his joy;
The Youth, who daily farther from the east
Must travel, still is Nature's Priest,
And by the vision splendid
Is on his way attended;
At length the Man perceives it die away,
And fade into the light of common day.

Earth fills her lap with pleasures of her own;
Yearnings she hath in her own natural kind,
And, even with something of a Mother's mind,
And no unworthy aim,
The homely Nurse doth all she can
To make her Foster-child, her Inmate Man,
Forget the glories he hath known,
And that imperial palace whence he came.

Behold the Child among his new-born blisses,
A six years' Darling of a pigmy size!
See, where 'mid work of his own hand he lies,
Fretted by sallies of his mother's kisses,
With light upon him from his father's eyes!
See, at his feet, some little plan or chart,
Some fragment from his dream of human life,
Shaped by himself with newly-learned art;
A wedding or a festival,
A mourning or a funeral;
And this hath now his heart,
And unto this he frames his song:
Then will he fit his tongue
To dialogues of business, love, or strife;
But it will not be long
Ere this be thrown aside,
And with new joy and pride
The little Actor cons another part;
Filling from time to time his "humorous stage"
With all the Persons, down to palsied Age,
That Life brings with her in her equipage;
As if his whole vocation
Were endless imitation.

Thou, whose exterior semblance doth belie
Thy Soul's immensity;
Thou best Philosopher, who yet dost keep
Thy heritage, thou Eye among the blind,
That, deaf and silent, read'st the eternal deep,

1804

Haunted for ever by the eternal mind,—
        Mighty Prophet! Seer blest!
        On whom those truths do rest,
Which we are toiling all our lives to find,
In darkness lost, the darkness of the grave;
Thou, over whom thy Immortality
Broods like the Day, a Master o'er a Slave,
A Presence which is not to be put by;
Thou little Child, yet glorious in the might
Of heaven-born freedom on thy being's height,
Why with such earnest pains dost thou provoke
The years to bring the inevitable yoke,
Thus blindly with thy blessedness at strife?
Full soon thy Soul shall have her earthly freight,
And custom lie upon thee with a weight,
Heavy as frost, and deep almost as life!

        O joy! that in our embers
        Is something that doth live,
        That Nature yet remembers
        What was so fugitive!
The thought of our past years in me doth breed
Perpetual benediction: not indeed
For that which is most worthy to be blest—
Delight and liberty, the simple creed
Of Childhood, whether busy or at rest,

1804

With new-fledged hope still fluttering in his breast:—
        Not for these I raise
        The song of thanks and praise
        But for those obstinate questionings
        Of sense and outward things,
        Fallings from us, vanishings;
        Blank misgivings of a Creature
Moving about in worlds not realised,
High instincts before which our mortal Nature
Did tremble like a guilty Thing surprised:
        But for those first affections,
        Those shadowy recollections,
        Which, be they what they may
Are yet the fountain-light of all our day,
Are yet a master-light of all our seeing;
        Uphold us, cherish, and have power to make
Our noisy years seem moments in the being
Of the eternal Silence: truths that wake,
        To perish never;
Which neither listlessness, nor mad endeavour,
        Nor Man nor Boy,
Nor all that is at enmity with joy,

Can utterly abolish or destroy!
             Hence in a season of calm weather
             Though inland far we be,
Our Souls have sight of that immortal sea
             Which brought us hither,
             Can in a moment travel thither,
And see the Children sport upon the shore,
And hear the mighty waters rolling evermore.

Then sing, ye Birds, sing, sing a joyous song!
             And let the young Lambs bound
             As to the tabor's sound!
We in thought will join your throng,
             Ye that pipe and ye that play,
             Ye that through your hearts to-day
             Feel the gladness of the May!
What though the radiance which was once so bright
Be now for ever taken from my sight,
    Though nothing can bring back the hour
Of splendour in the grass, of glory in the flower;
             We will grieve not, rather find
             Strength in what remains behind;
             In the primal sympathy
             Which having been must ever be;
             In the soothing thoughts that spring
             Out of human suffering;
             In the faith that looks through death,
In years that bring the philosophic mind.

And O, ye Fountains, Meadows, Hills, and Groves,
Forebode not any severing of our loves!
Yet in my heart of hearts I feel your might;
I only have relinquished one delight
To live beneath your more habitual sway.
I love the Brooks which down their channels fret,
Even more than when I tripped lightly as they;
The innocent brightness of a new-born Day
             Is lovely yet;
The Clouds that gather round the setting sun
Do take a sober colouring from an eye
That hath kept watch o'er man's mortality;
Another race hath been, and other palms are won.
Thanks to the human heart by which we live,
Thanks to its tenderness, its joys, and fears,
To me the meanest flower that blows can give
Thoughts that do often lie too deep for tears.

1804

THE BARD'S INCANTATION
(WRITTEN UNDER THREAT OF AN INVASION IN THE AUTUMN OF 1804)

Sir Walter Scott

The Forest of Glenmore is drear,
   It is all of black pine, and the dark oak-tree;
And the midnight wind, to the mountain deer,
   Is whistling the forest lullaby:
The moon looks through the drifting storm,
But the troubled lake reflects not her form,
For the waves roll whitening to the land,
And dash against the shelvy strand.

There is a voice among the trees,
   That mingles with the groaning oak—
That mingles with the stormy breeze,
   And the lake-waves dashing against the rock;—
There is a voice within the wood,
The voice of the Bard in fitful mood;
His song was louder than the blast,
As the Bard of Glenmore through the forest past.

"Wake ye from your sleep of death,
   Minstrels and bards of other days!
For the midnight wind is on the heath,
   And the midnight meteors dimly blaze:
The Spectre with his Bloody Hand,[12]
Is wandering through the wild woodland;
The owl and the raven are mute for dread,
And the time is meet to awake the dead!

"Souls of the mighty, wake, and say
   To what high strain your harps were strung,
When Lochlin plough'd her billowy way,
   And on your shores her Norsemen flung?
Her Norsemen train'd to spoil and blood,
Skill'd to prepare the Raven's food,
All, by your harpings, doom'd to die
On bloody Largs and Loncarty.[13]

1804

12 Author's note: "The forest of Glenmore is haunted by a spirit called Lham-dearg, or Red-hand." Labraid Lámh Dhearg is a mythical Irish figure from the Fenian (also known as Ossianic) Cycle. The Red Hand of Ulster, a symbol of the Irish province of Ulster, is said to originate from him.
13 Author's note: "Where the Norwegian invader of Scotland received two bloody defeats." The reference is to the battles of Luncarty (990) and Largs (1263).

"Mute are ye all? No murmurs strange
    Upon the midnight breeze sail by;
Nor through the pines, with whistling change,
    Mimic the harp's wild harmony!
Mute are ye now?—Ye ne'er were mute,
When Murder with his bloody foot,
And Rapine with his iron hand,
Were hovering near yon mountain strand.

"O yet awake the strain to tell,
    By every deed in song enroll'd,
By every chief who fought or fell
    For Albion's weal in battle bold;—
From Coilgach,[14] first, who rolled his car,
Through the deep ranks of Roman war,
To him, of veteran memory dear,
Who, victor, died on Aboukir.

"By all their swords, by all their scars,
    By all their names, a mighty spell!
By all their wounds, by all their wars,
    Arise, the mighty strain to tell!
For fiercer than fierce Hengist's strain,
More impious than the heathen Dane,
More grasping than all-grasping Rome,
Gaul's ravening legions hither come!"—

The wind is hush'd, and still the lake—
    Strange murmurs fill my tinkling ears,
Bristles my hair, my sinews quake,
    At the dread voice of other years—
"When targets clash'd, and bugles rung,
And blades round warriors' heads were flung,
The foremost of the band were we,
And hymn'd the joys of Liberty!"

1804

---

14 Author's note: "The Galgacus of Tacitus." Calgacus or Galgacus
was a Caledonian chieftain who fought against Roman invaders in
AD 83 or 84.

1805

MY NATIVE LAND
(from *Lay of the Last Minstrel* Canto 6)

Sir Walter Scott

Breathes there the man, with soul so dead,
Who never to himself hath said,
    This is my own, my native land!
Whose heart hath ne'er within him burn'd,
As home his footsteps he hath turn'd
    From wandering on a foreign strand!
If such there breathe, go, mark him well;
For him no Minstrel raptures swell;
High though his titles, proud his name,
Boundless his wealth as wish can claim;
Despite those titles, power, and pelf,
The wretch, concentred all in self,
Living, shall forfeit fair renown,
And, doubly dying, shall go down
To the vile dust, from whence he sprung,
Unwept, unhonoured, and unsung.

1805

1806

THE PALMER
Sir Walter Scott

"O, open the door, some pity to show,
  Keen blows the northern wind!
The glen is white with the drifted snow,
  And the path is hard to find.

"No outlaw seeks your castle gate,
  From chasing the King's deer,
Though even an outlaw's wretched state
  Might claim compassion here.

"A weary Palmer, worn and weak,
  I wander for my sin;
O, open, for Our Lady's sake!
  A pilgrim's blessing win!

"I'll give you pardons from the Pope,
  And reliques from o'er the sea,—
Or if for these you will not ope,
  Yet open for charity.

"The hare is crouching in her form,
  The hart beside the hind;
An aged man, amid the storm,
  No shelter can I find.

"You hear the Ettrick's sullen roar,
  Dark, deep, and strong is he,
And I must ford the Ettrick o'er,
  Unless you pity me.

"The iron gate is bolted hard,
  At which I knock in vain;
The owner's heart is closer barr'd,
  Who hears me thus complain.

"Farewell, farewell! and Mary grant,
  When old and frail you be,
You never may the shelter want,
  That's now denied to me."

The Ranger on his couch lay warm,
  And heard him plead in vain;
But oft amid December's storm,
  He'll hear that voice again:

For lo, when through the vapours dank,
  Morn shone on Ettrick fair,
A corpse amid the alders rank,
  The Palmer welter'd there.

1807

THE HARP THAT ONCE THROUGH TARA'S HALLS
Thomas Moore

The harp that once through Tara's halls
   The soul of music shed,
Now hangs as mute on Tara's walls,
   As if that soul were fled.—
So sleeps the pride of former days,
   So glory's thrill is o'er,
And hearts, that once beat high for praise,
   Now feel that pulse no more.

No more to chiefs and ladies bright
   The harp of Tara swells;
The chord alone, that breaks at night,
   Its tale of ruin tells.
Thus Freedom now so seldom wakes,
   The only throb she gives,
Is when some heart indignant breaks,
   To show that still she lives.

1807

1808

Preface to **"MILTON"**
William Blake

And did those feet in ancient time,
Walk upon Englands mountains green:
And was the holy Lamb of God,
On Englands pleasant pastures seen!

And did the Countenance Divine
Shine forth upon our clouded hills?
And was Jerusalem builded here,
Among these dark Satanic Mills?

Bring me my Bow of burning gold:
Bring me my Arrows of desire:
Bring me my Spear: O clouds unfold!
Bring me my Chariot of fire!

I will not cease from Mental Fight,
Nor shall my Sword sleep in my hand:
Till we have built Jerusalem,
In Englands green & pleasant Land.

1810

WRITTEN AFTER SWIMMING
FROM SESTOS TO ABYDOS

George Gordon, Lord Byron

If in the month of dark December,
   Leander, who was nightly wont
(What maid will not the tale remember?)
   To cross thy stream, broad Hellespont!

If, when the wintry tempest roar'd,
   He sped to Hero, nothing loth,
And thus of old thy current pour'd,
   Fair Venus! how I pity both!

For *me*, degenerate modern wretch,
   Though in the genial month of May,
My dripping limbs I faintly stretch,
   And think I've done a feat to-day.

But since he cross'd the rapid tide,
   According to the doubtful story,
To woo,—and—Lord knows what beside,
And swam for Love, as I for Glory;

'Twere hard to say who fared the best:
   Sad mortals! thus the Gods still plague you!
He lost his labour, I my jest:
   For he was drown'd, and I've the ague.

1810

1812

THE BOLD DRAGOON (A SONG)
Sir Walter Scott

'Twas a Maréchal of France, and he fain would honour gain,
And he long'd to take a passing glance at Portugal from Spain;
    With his flying guns this gallant gay,
    And boasted corps d'armée—
O he fear'd not our dragoons, with their long swords, boldly riding,
    Whack, fal de ral, &c.

To Campo Mayor come, he had quietly sat down,
Just a fricassee to pick, while his soldiers sack'd the town,
    When, 'twas peste! morblue! mon General,
    Hear the English bugle-call!
And behold the light dragoons, with their long swords, boldly riding,
    Whack, fal de ral, &c.

Right about went horse and foot, artillery and all,
And, as the devil leaves a house, they tumbled through the wall;
    They took no time to seek the door,
    But, best foot set before—
O they ran from our dragoons, with their long swords, boldy riding,
    Whack, fal de ral, &c.

Those valiant men of France they had scarcely fled a mile,
When on their flank there sous'd at one the British rank and file;
    For Long, De Grey, and Otway, then
    Ne'er minded one to ten,
But came on like light dragoons, with their long swords, boldly riding,
    Whack, fal de ral, &c.

Three hundred British lads they made three thousand reel,
Their hearts were made of English oak, their swords of Sheffield steel,
    Their horses were in Yorkshire bred,
    And Beresford them led;
So huzza for brave dragoons, with their long swords, boldly riding,
    Whack, fal de ral, &c.

Then here's a health to Wellington, to Beresford, to Long,
And a single word of Bonaparte before I close my song:
    The eagles that to fight he brings
    Should serve his men with wings,
When they meet the bold dragoons, with their long swords, boldly
                                    riding,
    Whack, fal de ral, &c.

1814

SHE WALKS IN BEAUTY
George Gordon, Lord Byron

She walks in beauty, like the night
    Of cloudless climes and starry skies;
And all that's best of dark and bright
    Meet in her aspect and her eyes:
Thus mellow'd to that tender light
    Which heaven to gaudy day denies.

One shade the more, one ray the less,
    Had half impair'd the nameless grace
Which waves in every raven tress,
    Or softly lightens o'er her face;
Where thoughts serenely sweet express
    How pure, how dear their dwelling place.

And on that cheek, and o'er that brow,
    So soft, so calm, yet eloquent,
The smiles that win, the tints that glow,
    But tell of days in goodness spent,
A mind at peace with all below,
    A heart whose love is innocent!

TO BYRON
John Keats

Byron! how sweetly sad thy melody!
    Attuning still the soul to tenderness,
    As if soft Pity, with unusual stress,
Had touch'd her plaintive lute, and thou, being by,
Hadst caught the tones, nor suffer'd them to die.
    O'ershadowing sorrow doth not make thee less
    Delightful: thou thy griefs dost dress
With a bright halo, shining beamily,
As when a cloud the golden moon doth veil,
    Its sides are ting'd with a resplendent glow,
Through the dark robe oft amber rays prevail,
    And like fair veins in sable marble flow;
Still warble, dying swan! still tell the tale,
    The enchanting tale, the tale of pleasing woe.

1815

TO WORDSWORTH
Percy Shelley

Poet of Nature, thou hast wept to know
That things depart which never may return;
Childhood and youth, friendship and love's first glow,
Have fled like sweet dreams, leaving thee to mourn.
These common woes I feel. One loss is mine,
Which thou too feel'st; yet I alone deplore.
Thou wert as a lone star, whose light did shine
On some frail bark in winter's midnight roar:
Thou hast like to a rock-built refuge stood
Above the blind and battling multitude:
In honoured poverty thy voice did weave
Songs consecrate to truth and liberty,—
Deserting these, thou leavest me to grieve,
Thus having been, that thou shouldst cease to be.

1815

WRITTEN ON THE DAY
THAT MR LEIGH HUNT LEFT PRISON
John Keats

What though, for showing truth to flatter'd state,
    Kind Hunt was shut in prison, yet has he,
    In his immortal spirit, been as free
As the sky-searching lark, and as elate.
Minion of grandeur! think you he did wait?
    Think you he nought but prison walls did see,
    Till, so unwilling, thou unturn'dst the key?
Ah, no! far happier, nobler was his fate!
In Spenser's halls he stray'd, and bowers fair,
    Culling enchanted flowers; and he flew
With daring Milton through the fields of air:
    To regions of his own his genius true
Took happy flights. Who shall his fame impair,
When thou art dead, and all thy wretched crew?

NATIONAL SONG
James Henry Leigh Hunt

Hail, England, dear England, true Queen of the West,
With thy fair swelling bosom and ever-green vest,
How nobly thou sitt'st in thine own steady light,
On the left of thee Freedom, and Truth on the right,
While the clouds, at thy smile, break apart, and turn bright!
The Muses, full voiced, half encircle the seat,
And Ocean comes kissing thy princely white feet.
      All hail! All hail!
All hail to the beauty, immortal and free,
The only true goddess that rose from the sea.

Warm-hearted, high-thoughted, what union is thine
Of gentle affections and genius divine!
Thy sons are true men, fit to battle with care;
Thy daughters true women, home-loving and fair,
With figures unequall'd, and blushes as rare:
E'en the ground takes a virtue, that's trodden by thee,
And the slave, that but touches it, starts, and is free.
      All hail! All hail!
All hail, Queen of Queens, there's no monarch beside,
But in ruling as thou dost, would double his pride.

1815

WHEN WE TWO PARTED
George Gordon, Lord Byron

When we two parted
  In silence and tears,
Half broken-hearted
  To sever for years,
Pale grew thy cheek and cold,
  Colder thy kiss;
Truly that hour foretold
  Sorrow to this.

The dew of the morning
  Sunk chill on my brow—
It felt like the warning
  Of what I feel now.
Thy vows are all broken,
  And light is thy fame;
I hear thy name spoken,
  And share in its shame.

They name thee before me,
   A knell to mine ear;
A shudder comes o'er me—
   Why wert thou so dear?
They know not I knew thee,
   Who knew thee too well:—
Long, long shall I rue thee,
   Too deeply to tell.

In secret we met—
   In silence I grieve,
That thy heart could forget,
   Thy spirit deceive.
If I should meet thee
   After long years,
How should I greet thee!—
   With silence and tears.

FEELINGS OF A REPUBLICAN ON THE FALL OF BONAPARTE
Percy Shelley

1815

I hated thee, fallen tyrant! I did groan
To think that a most unambitious slave,
Like thou, shouldst dance and revel on the grave
Of Liberty. Thou mightst have built thy throne
Where it had stood even now: thou didst prefer
A frail and bloody pomp, which Time has swept
In fragments towards Oblivion. Massacre,
For this I prayed, would on thy sleep have crept,
Treason and Slavery, Rapine, Fear, and Lust,
And stifled thee, their minister. I know
Too late, since thou and France are in the dust,
That Virtue owns a more eternal foe
Than Force or Fraud: old Custom, legal Crime,
And bloody Faith, the foulest birth of Time.

1816

MUTABILITY
Percy Shelley

We are as clouds that veil the midnight moon;
   How restlessly they speed and gleam, and quiver,
Streaking the darkness radiantly!—yet soon
   Night closes round, and they are lost for ever:

Or like forgotten lyres, whose dissonant strings
   Give various response to each varying blast,
To whose frail frame no second motion brings
   One mood or modulation like the last.

We rest.—A dream has power to poison sleep;
   We rise.—One wandering thought pollutes the day;
We feel, conceive or reason, laugh or weep;
   Embrace fond woe, or cast our cares away:

It is the same!—For, be it joy or sorrow,
   The path of its departure still is free:
Man's yesterday may ne'er be like his morrow;
   Nought may endure but Mutability.

1816

HYMN TO INTELLECTUAL BEAUTY
Percy Shelley

The awful shadow of some unseen Power
   Floats tho' unseen among us; visiting
   This various world with as inconstant wing
As summer winds that creep from flower to flower;
Like moonbeams that behind some piny mountain shower,
     It visits with inconstant glance
     Each human heart and countenance;
Like hues and harmonies of evening,
     Like clouds in starlight widely spread,
     Like memory of music fled,
     Like aught that for its grace may be
Dear, and yet dearer for its mystery.—

Spirit of BEAUTY, that dost consecrate
　　With thine own hues all thou dost shine upon
　　Of human thought or form, where art thou gone?
Why dost thou pass away and leave our state,
This dim vast vale of tears, vacant and desolate?
　　　Ask why the sunlight not for ever
　　　Weaves rainbows o'er yon mountain river;
Why aught should fail and fade that once is shown;
　　Why fear and dream and death and birth
　　Cast on the daylight of this earth
　　Such gloom; why man has such a scope
For love and hate, despondency and hope;

No voice from some sublimer world hath ever
　　To sage or poet these responses given:
　　Therefore the names of Demon, Ghost, and Heaven,
Remain the records of their vain endeavour;
Frail spells whose uttered charm might not avail to sever,
　　From all we hear and all we see,
　　Doubt, chance, and mutability.
Thy light alone like mist o'er mountains driven,
　　Or music by the night wind sent
　　Through strings of some still instrument,
　　Or moonlight on a midnight stream,
Gives grace and truth to life's unquiet dream.

1816

Love, Hope, and Self-esteem, like clouds, depart
　　And come, for some uncertain moments lent.
　　Man were immortal and omnipotent,
Didst thou, unknown and awful as thou art,
Keep with thy glorious train firm state within his heart.
　　Thou messenger of sympathies,
　　That wax and wane in lovers' eyes;
Thou, that to human thought art nourishment,
　　Like darkness to a dying flame!
　　Depart not as thy shadow came;
　　Depart not, lest the grave should be,
　　Like life and fear, a dark reality.

While yet a boy I sought for ghosts, and sped
　　Thro' many a listening chamber, cave, and ruin,
　　And starlight wood, with fearful steps pursuing
Hopes of high talk with the departed dead.
I called on poisonous names with which our youth is fed:
　　I was not heard, I saw them not;
　　When musing deeply on the lot

Of life, at that sweet time when winds are wooing
   All vital things that wake to bring
   News of birds and blossoming,
   Sudden, thy shadow fell on me;
 I shrieked, and clasped my hands in ecstasy!

I vowed that I would dedicate my powers
   To thee and thine: have I not kept the vow?
   With beating heart and streaming eyes, even now
I call the phantoms of a thousand hours
Each from his voiceless grave: they have in visioned bowers
   Of studious zeal or love's delight
   Outwatched with me the envious night:
They know that never joy illumed my brow
   Unlinked with hope that thou wouldst free
   This world from its dark slavery,
   That thou, O awful LOVELINESS,
Wouldst give whate'er these words cannot express.

The day becomes more solemn and serene
   When noon is past: there is a harmony
   In autumn, and a lustre in its sky,
Which thro' the summer is not heard nor seen,
As if it could not be, as if it had not been!
   Thus let thy power, which like the truth   1816
   Of nature on my passive youth
Descended, to my onward life supply
   Its calm, to one who worships thee,
   And every form containing thee,
   Whom, SPIRIT fair, thy spells did bind
To fear himself, and love all human kind.

THE PAINS OF SLEEP

Samuel Taylor Coleridge

Ere on my bed my limbs I lay,
It hath not been my use to pray
With moving lips or bended knees;
But silently, by slow degrees,
My spirit I to Love compose,
In humble Trust mine eye-lids close,
With reverential resignation,
No wish conceived, no thought expressed!
Only a *sense* of supplication,

A sense o'er all my soul imprest
That I am weak, yet not unblest,
Since in me, round me, every where
Eternal Strength and Wisdom are.

But yester-night I pray'd aloud
In anguish and in agony,
Up-starting from the fiendish crowd
Of shapes and thoughts that tortured me:
A lurid light, a trampling throng,
Sense of intolerable wrong,
And whom I scorn'd, those only strong!
Thirst of revenge, the powerless will
Still baffled, and yet burning still!
Desire with loathing strangely mixed
On wild or hateful objects fixed.
Fantastic passions! mad'ning brawl!
And shame and terror over all!
Deeds to be hid which were not hid,
Which all confused I could not know,
Whether I suffered, or I did:
For all seemed guilt, remorse or woe,
My own or others still the same
Life-stifling fear, soul-stifling shame!

1816

So two nights passed: the night's dismay
Sadden'd and stunn'd the coming day.
Sleep, the wide blessing, seemed to me
Distemper's worst calamity.
The third night, when my own loud scream
Had waked me from the fiendish dream,
O'ercome with sufferings strange and wild,
I wept as I had been a child;
And having thus by tears subdued
My anguish to a milder mood,
Such punishments, I said, were due
To natures deepliest stain'd with sin:
For aye entempesting anew
Th' unfathomable hell within
The horror of their deeds to view,
To know and loathe, yet wish and do!
Such griefs with such men well agree,
But wherefore, wherefore fall on me?
To be loved is all I need,
And whom I love, I love indeed.

FARE THEE WELL
George Gordon, Lord Byron

"Alas! they had been friends in youth:
But whispering tongues can poison truth;
And constancy lives in realms above;
And life is thorny; and youth is vain;
And to be wroth with one we love,
Doth work like madness in the brain;

———————

WBut never either found another
To free the hollow heart from paining –
They stood aloof, the scars remaining.
Like cliffs which had been rent asunder;
A dreary sea now flows between,
But neither heat, nor frost, nor thunder,
Shall wholly do away, I ween,
The marks of that which once hath been."
from Coleridge, *Christabel*

Fare thee well! and if for ever,
   Still for ever, fare *thee well*:
Even though unforgiving, never
   'Gainst thee shall my heart rebel.

1816

Would that breast were bared before thee
   Where thy head so oft hath lain,
While that placid sleep came o'er thee
   Which thou ne'er canst know again:

Would that breast, by thee glanced over,
   Every inmost thought could show!
Then thou wouldst at last discover
   'Twas not well to spurn it so.

Though the world for this commend thee—
   Though it smile upon the blow,
Even its praises must offend thee,
   Founded on another's woe—

Though my many faults defaced me,
   Could no other arm be found
Than the one which once embraced me,
   To inflict a cureless wound?

Yet, oh yet, thyself deceive not;
   Love may sink by slow decay,
But by sudden wrench, believe not
   Hearts can thus be torn away:

Still thine own its life retaineth—
   Still must mine, though bleeding, beat;
And the undying thought which paineth
   Is—that we no more may meet.

These are words of deeper sorrow
   Than the wail above the dead;
Both shall live, but every morrow
   Wake us from a widowed bed.

And when thou wouldst solace gather,
   When our child's first accents flow,
Wilt thou teach her to say "Father!"
   Though his care she must forego?

When her little hands shall press thee,
   When her lip to thine is prest,
Think of him whose prayer shall bless thee,
   Think of him thy love had bless'd!

Should her lineaments resemble
   Those thou never more may'st see,
Then thy heart will softly tremble
   With a pulse yet true to me.

All my faults perchance thou knowest,
   All my madness none can know;
All my hopes, where'er thou goest,
   Wither—yet with *thee* they go.

Every feeling hath been shaken;
   Pride, which not a world could bow,
Bows to thee—by thee forsaken,
   Even my soul forsakes me now:

But 'tis done—all words are idle—
   Words from me are vainer still;
But the thoughts we cannot bridle
   Force their way without the will.—

Fare thee well!—thus disunited,
   Torn from every nearer tie,
Seared in heart, and lone, and blighted—
   More than this I scarce can die.

1816

PROMETHEUS
George Gordon, Lord Byron

Titan! to whose immortal eyes
    The sufferings of mortality,
    Seen in their sad reality,
Were not as things that gods despise;
What was thy pity's recompense?
A silent suffering, and intense;
The rock, the vulture, and the chain,
All that the proud can feel of pain,
The agony they do not show,
The suffocating sense of woe,
    Which speaks but in its loneliness,
And then is jealous lest the sky
Should have a listener, nor will sigh
    Until its voice is echoless.

Titan! to thee the strife was given
    Between the suffering and the will,
    Which torture where they cannot kill;
And the inexorable Heaven,
And the deaf tyranny of Fate,
The ruling principle of Hate,
Which for its pleasure doth create
The things it may annihilate,
Refus'd thee even the boon to die:
The wretched gift eternity
    Was thine—and thou hast borne it well.
All that the Thunderer wrung from thee
Was but the menace which flung back
On him the torments of thy rack;
The fate thou didst so well foresee,
But wouldst not to appease him tell;
And in thy silence was his sentence,
And in his soul a vain repentance,
And evil dread so ill dissembled
That in his hand the lightnings trembled.

Thy Godlike crime was to be kind,
    To render with thy precepts less
    The sum of human wretchedness,

1816

115

And strengthen Man with his own mind;
But baffled as thou wert from high,
Still in thy patient energy,
In the endurance, and repulse
   Of thine impenetrable spirit,
Which Earth and Heaven could not convulse,
   A mighty lesson we inherit:
Thou art a symbol and a sign
   To mortals of their fate and force;
Like thee, Man is in part divine,
   A troubled stream from a pure source;
And Man in portions can foresee
His own funereal destiny;
His wretchedness, and his resistance,
And his sad unallied existence:
To which his spirit may oppose
Itself—and equal to all woes,
   And a firm will, and a deep sense,
Which even in torture can descry
   Its own concentred recompense,
Triumphant where it dares defy,
And making death a victory.

1816

TO ONE WHO HAS BEEN LONG IN CITY PENT
John Keats

To one who has been long in city pent,
   'Tis very sweet to look into the fair
   And open face of heaven,—to breathe a prayer
Full in the smile of the blue firmament.
Who is more happy, when, with heart's content,
   Fatigued he sinks into some pleasant lair
   Of wavy grass, and reads a debonair
And gentle tale of love and languishment?
Returning home at evening, with an ear
   Catching the notes of Philomel,—an eye
Watching the sailing cloudlet's bright career,
   He mourns that day so soon has glided by:
E'en like the passage of an angel's tear
   That falls through the clear ether silently.

ON FIRST LOOKING INTO CHAPMAN'S HOMER
John Keats

Much have I travell'd in the realms of gold,
   And many goodly states and kingdoms seen;
   Round many western islands have I been
Which bards in fealty to Apollo hold.
Oft of one wide expanse had I been told
   That deep-brow'd Homer rul'd as his demesne;
   Yet did I never breathe its pure serene
Till I heard Chapman speak out loud and bold:
Then felt I like some watcher of the skies
   When a new planet swims into his ken;
Or like stout Cortez when with eagle eyes
   He star'd at the Pacific—and all his men
Look'd at each other with a wild surmise —
   Silent, upon a peak in Darien.

1816

1817

OZYMANDIAS
Percy Shelley

I met a traveller from an antique land,
Who said: "Two vast and trunkless legs of stone
Stand in the desert. Near them, on the sand,
Half sunk, a shattered visage lies, whose frown,
And wrinkled lip, and sneer of cold command,
Tell that its sculptor well those passions read
Which yet survive, stamped on these lifeless things,
The hand that mocked them and the heart that fed;
And on the pedestal these words appear:
'My name is Ozymandias, King of Kings:
Look on my Works, ye Mighty, and despair!'
Nothing beside remains. Round the decay
Of that colossal Wreck, boundless and bare,
The lone and level sands stretch far away."

1817

ON SEEING THE ELGIN MARBLES
John Keats

My spirit is too weak—mortality
    Weighs heavily on me like unwilling sleep,
    And each imagin'd pinnacle and steep
Of godlike hardship tells me I must die
Like a sick Eagle looking at the sky.
    Yet 'tis a gentle luxury to weep
    That I have not the cloudy winds to keep,
Fresh for the opening of the morning's eye.
Such dim-conceived glories of the brain
    Bring round the heart an undescribable feud;
So do these wonders a most dizzy pain,
    That mingles Grecian grandeur with the rude
Wasting of old Time—with a billowy main—
    A sun—a shadow of a magnitude.

ON THE DEATH OF PRINCESS CHARLOTTE
Anna Laetitia Barbauld

Yes—Britain mourns; as with electric touch
For youth, for love, for happiness destroyed,
Her universal population melts
In grief spontaneous, and hard hearts are moved,
And rough unpolished natures learn to feel
For those they envied, levelled in the dust
By Fate's impartial stroke, and pulpits sound
With vanity and woe to earthly goods,
And urge and dry the tear.—Yet one there is
Who 'midst this general burst of grief remains
In strange tranquillity. Whom not the stir
And long-drawn murmurs of the gathering crowd,
That by his very windows trail the pomp
Of hearse, and blazoned arms, and long array
Of sad funereal rites, nor the loud groans,
And deep-felt anguish of a husband's heart,
Can move to mingle with this flood one tear.
In careless apathy, perhaps in mirth,
He wears the day. Yet is he near in blood,
The very stem on which this blossom grew,
And at his knees she fondled in the charm,
And grace spontaneous, which alone belongs
To untaught infancy.—Yet oh forbear,
Nor deem him hard of heart: for, awful, struck
By heaven's severest visitation, sad,
Like a scathed oak amidst the forest trees,
Lonely he stands; leaves bud, and shoot, and fall;
He holds no sympathy with living nature,
Or time's incessant change. Then in this hour,
While pensive thought is busy with the woes
And restless change of poor humanity,
Think then, oh think of him, and breathe one prayer,
From the full tide of sorrow spare one tear,
For him who does not weep.

1817

1818

SONNET: LIFT NOT THE PAINTED VEIL
Percy Shelley

Lift not the painted veil which those who live
Call Life: though unreal shapes be pictured there,
And it but mimic all we would believe
With colours idly spread,—behind, lurk Fear
And Hope, twin Destinies; who ever weave
Their shadows, o'er the chasm, sightless and drear.

I knew one who had lifted it—he sought,
For his lost heart was tender, things to love,
But found them not, alas! nor was there aught
The world contains, the which he could approve.
Through the unheeding many he did move,
A splendour among shadows, a bright blot
Upon this gloomy scene, a Spirit that strove
For truth, and like the Preacher found it not.

1818

ON SITTING DOWN TO READ KING LEAR ONCE AGAIN
John Keats

O golden-tongued Romance with serene lute!
    Fair plumed Syren! Queen of far-away!
    Leave melodizing on this wintry day,
Shut up thine olden pages, and be mute:
Adieu! for, once again, the fierce dispute,
    Betwixt damnation and impassion'd clay
    Must I burn through; once more humbly assay
The bitter-sweet of this Shakespearian fruit:
Chief Poet! and ye clouds of Albion,
    Begetters of our deep eternal theme!
When through the old oak Forest I am gone,
    Let me not wander in a barren dream,
But, when I am consumed in the fire,
Give me new Phoenix wings to fly at my desire.

WHEN I HAVE FEARS THAT I MAY CEASE TO BE
John Keats

When I have fears that I may cease to be
   Before my pen has glean'd my teeming brain,
Before high-pilèd books, in charactery,
   Hold like rich garners the full ripened grain;
When I behold, upon the night's starr'd face,
   Huge cloudy symbols of a high romance,
And think that I may never live to trace
   Their shadows, with the magic hand of chance;
And when I feel, fair creature of an hour,
   That I shall never look upon thee more,
Never have relish in the faery power
   Of unreflecting love;—then on the shore
Of the wide world I stand alone, and think
Till love and fame to nothingness do sink.

ON RECEIVING A CROWN OF IVY FROM JOHN KEATS
James Henry Leigh Hunt

1818

It is a lofty feeling, yet a kind,
Thus to be topped with leaves;—to have a sense
Of honour-shaded thought,—an influence
As from great Nature's fingers, and be twined
With her old, sacred, verdurous ivy-bind,
As though she hallowed with that sylvan fence
A head that bows to her benevolence,
Midst pomp of fancied trumpets in the wind.
'Tis what's within us crowned. And kind and great
Are all the conquering wishes it inspires,—
Love of things lasting, love of the tall woods,
Love of love's self, and ardour for a state
Of natural good befitting such desires,
Towns without gain, and hunted solitudes.

1819

LA BELLE DAME SANS MERCI: A BALLAD
John Keats

O what can ail thee, knight-at-arms,
   Alone and palely loitering?
The sedge has wither'd from the lake,
   And no birds sing.

O what can ail thee, knight-at-arms!
   So haggard and so woe-begone?
The squirrel's granary is full,
   And the harvest's done.

I see a lily on thy brow,
   With anguish moist and fever dew,
And on thy cheeks a fading rose
   Fast withereth too.

I met a lady in the meads,
   Full beautiful—a faery's child,
Her hair was long, her foot was light,
   And her eyes were wild.

I made a garland for her head,
   And bracelets too, and fragrant zone;
She look'd at me as she did love,
   And made sweet moan.

I set her on my pacing steed,
   And nothing else saw all day long,
For sidelong would she bend, and sing
   A faery's song.

She found me roots of relish sweet,
   And honey wild, and manna dew,
And sure in language strange she said —
   "I love thee true."

She took me to her elfin grot,
   And there she wept, and sigh'd full sore,
And there I shut her wild wild eyes
   With kisses four.

And there she lullèd me asleep,
   And there I dream'd—Ah! woe betide!
The latest dream I ever dream'd
   On the cold hill's side.

I saw pale kings and princes too,
   Pale warriors, death-pale were they all;
They cried—"La Belle Dame sans Merci
   Hath thee in thrall!"

I saw their starved lips in the gloam,
   With horrid warning gapèd wide,
And I awoke and found me here,
   On the cold hill's side.

And this is why I sojourn here,
   Alone and palely loitering,
Though the sedge is wither'd from the lake,
   And no birds sing.

1819

TO SLEEP

John Keats

O soft embalmer of the still midnight!
   Shutting, with careful fingers and benign,
Our gloom-pleased eyes, embower'd from the light,
   Enshaded in forgetfulness divine;
O soothest Sleep! if so it please thee, close
   In midst of this thine hymn, my willing eyes,
Or wait the amen, ere thy poppy throws
   Around my bed its lulling charities;
Then save me, or the passed day will shine
Upon my pillow, breeding many woes;
   Save me from curious conscience, that still lords
Its strength, for darkness burrowing like a mole;
   Turn the key deftly in the oiled wards,
And seal the hushed casket of my soul.

ODE TO A NIGHTINGALE

John Keats

My heart aches, and a drowsy numbness pains
   My sense, as though of hemlock I had drunk,
Or emptied some dull opiate to the drains
   One minute past, and Lethe-wards had sunk:
'Tis not through envy of thy happy lot,
   But being too happy in thine happiness,—
      That thou, light-winged Dryad of the trees
         In some melodious plot
Of beechen green, and shadows numberless,
   Singest of summer in full-throated ease.

O, for a draught of vintage! that hath been
   Cool'd a long age in the deep-delved earth,
Tasting of Flora and the country green,
   Dance, and Provençal song, and sunburnt mirth!
O for a beaker full of the warm South,
   Full of the true, the blushful Hippocrene,
      With beaded bubbles winking at the brim,
         And purple-stained mouth;
   That I might drink, and leave the world unseen,
      And with thee fade away into the forest dim:

Fade far away, dissolve, and quite forget
   What thou among the leaves hast never known,
The weariness, the fever, and the fret
   Here, where men sit and hear each other groan;
Where palsy shakes a few, sad, last gray hairs,
   Where youth grows pale, and spectre-thin, and dies;
      Where but to think is to be full of sorrow
         And leaden-ey'd despairs,
   Where Beauty cannot keep her lustrous eyes,
      Or new Love pine at them beyond to-morrow.

Away! away! for I will fly to thee,
   Not charioted by Bacchus and his pards,
But on the viewless wings of Poesy,
   Though the dull brain perplexes and retards:
Already with thee! tender is the night,
   And haply the Queen-Moon is on her throne,
      Cluster'd around by all her starry Fays;
         But here there is no light,

1819

Save what from heaven is with the breezes blown
   Through verdurous glooms and winding mossy ways.

I cannot see what flowers are at my feet,
   Nor what soft incense hangs upon the boughs,
But, in embalmed darkness, guess each sweet
   Wherewith the seasonable month endows
The grass, the thicket, and the fruit-tree wild;
   White hawthorn, and the pastoral eglantine;
     Fast fading violets cover'd up in leaves;
      And mid-May's eldest child,
   The coming musk-rose, full of dewy wine,
     The murmurous haunt of flies on summer eves.

Darkling I listen; and, for many a time
   I have been half in love with easeful Death,
Call'd him soft names in many a mused rhyme,
   To take into the air my quiet breath;
    Now more than ever seems it rich to die,
   To cease upon the midnight with no pain,
    While thou art pouring forth thy soul abroad
     In such an ecstasy!
   Still wouldst thou sing, and I have ears in vain—
    To thy high requiem become a sod.

Thou wast not born for death, immortal Bird!
   No hungry generations tread thee down;
The voice I hear this passing night was heard
   In ancient days by emperor and clown:
Perhaps the self-same song that found a path
   Through the sad heart of Ruth, when, sick for home,
    She stood in tears amid the alien corn;
     The same that oft-times hath
   Charm'd magic casements, opening on the foam
    Of perilous seas, in faery lands forlorn.

Forlorn! the very word is like a bell
   To toll me back from thee to my sole self!
Adieu! the fancy cannot cheat so well
   As she is fam'd to do, deceiving elf.
Adieu! adieu! thy plaintive anthem fades
   Past the near meadows, over the still stream,
    Up the hill-side; and now 'tis buried deep
     In the next valley-glades:
   Was it a vision, or a waking dream?
    Fled is that music:—Do I wake or sleep?

1819

BRIGHT STAR
John Keats

Bright star, would I were stedfast as thou art—
   Not in lone splendour hung aloft the night
And watching, with eternal lids apart,
   Like nature's patient, sleepless Eremite,
The moving waters at their priestlike task
   Of pure ablution round earth's human shores,
Or gazing on the new soft-fallen mask
   Of snow upon the mountains and the moors—
No—yet still stedfast, still unchangeable,
   Pillow'd upon my fair love's ripening breast,
To feel for ever its soft fall and swell,
   Awake for ever in a sweet unrest,
Still, still to hear her tender-taken breath,
And so live ever—or else swoon to death.

SONNET: ENGLAND IN 1819
1819   Percy Shelley

An old, mad, blind, despised, and dying King;
Princes, the dregs of their dull race, who flow
Through public scorn,—mud from a muddy spring;
Rulers who neither see nor feel nor know,
But leechlike to their fainting country cling
Till they drop, blind in blood, without a blow.
A people starved and stabbed in th' untilled field;
An army, whom liberticide and prey
Makes as a two-edged sword to all who wield;
Golden and sanguine laws which tempt and slay;
Religion Christless, Godless—a book sealed;
A senate, Time's worst statute, unrepealed—
Are graves from which a glorious Phantom may
Burst, to illumine our tempestuous day.

126

1820

TO A SKYLARK
Percy Shelley

Hail to thee, blithe Spirit!
  Bird thou never wert,
That from Heaven, or near it,
  Pourest thy full heart
In profuse strains of unpremeditated art.

Higher still and higher
  From the earth thou springest
Like a cloud of fire;
  The blue deep thou wingest,
And singing still dost soar, and soaring ever singest.

In the golden lightning
  Of the sunken sun,
O'er which clouds are bright'ning,
  Thou dost float and run;
Like an unbodied joy whose race is just begun.

1820

The pale purple even
  Melts around thy flight;
Like a star of Heaven,
  In the broad daylight
Thou art unseen, but yet I hear thy shrill delight,

Keen as are the arrows
  Of that silver sphere,
Whose intense lamp narrows
  In the white dawn clear,
Until we hardly see—we feel that it is there.

All the earth and air
  With thy voice is loud,
As, when night is bare,
  From one lonely cloud
The moon rains out her beams—and Heaven is overflowed.

What thou art we know not;
    What is most like thee?
From rainbow clouds there flow not
    Drops so bright to see
As from thy presence showers a rain of melody.

    Like a Poet hidden
        In the light of thought,
    Singing hymns unbidden,
        Till the world is wrought
To sympathy with hopes and fears it heeded not:

    Like a high-born maiden
        In a palace-tower,
    Soothing her love-laden
        Soul in secret hour,
With music sweet as love—which overflows her bower:

    Like a glow-worm golden
        In a dell of dew,
    Scattering unbeholden
        Its aereal hue
Among the flowers and grass, which screen it from the view:

    Like a rose embowered
        In its own green leaves,
    By warm winds deflowered—
        Till the scent it gives
Makes faint with too much sweet those heavy-wingèd thieves:

    Sound of vernal showers
        On the twinkling grass,
    Rain-awakened flowers,
        All that ever was
Joyous, and clear, and fresh, thy music doth surpass.

    Teach us, Sprite or Bird,
        What sweet thoughts are thine:
    I have never heard
        Praise of love or wine
That panted forth a flood of rapture so divine.

    Chorus Hymeneal,
        Or triumphal chant,
    Matched with thine would be all

But an empty vaunt,
A thing wherein we feel there is some hidden want.

What objects are the fountains
    Of thy happy strain?
What fields, or waves, or mountains?
    What shapes of sky or plain?
What love of thine own kind? what ignorance of pain?

With thy clear keen joyance
    Languor cannot be:
Shadow of annoyance
    Never came near thee:
Thou lovest: but ne'er knew love's sad satiety.

Waking or asleep,
    Thou of death must deem
Things more true and deep
    Than we mortals dream,
Or how could thy notes flow in such a crystal stream?

We look before and after,
    And pine for what is not:
Our sincerest laughter
    With some pain is fraught;
Our sweetest songs are those that tell of saddest thought.

Yet if we could scorn
    Hate, and pride, and fear;
If we were things born
    Not to shed a tear,
I know not how thy joy we ever should come near.

Better than all measures
    Of delightful sound,
Better than all treasures
    That in books are found,
Thy skill to poet were, thou Scorner of the ground!

Teach me half the gladness
    That thy brain must know,
Such harmonious madness
    From my lips would flow
The world should listen then, as I am listening now.

1820

SONG: MEN OF ENGLAND

Percy Shelley

Men of England, wherefore plough
For the lords who lay ye low?
Wherefore weave with toil and care
The rich robes your tyrants wear?

Wherefore feed and clothe and save
From the cradle to the grave
Those ungrateful drones who would
Drain your sweat—nay, drink your blood?

Wherefore, Bees of England, forge
Many a weapon, chain, and scourge,
That these stingless drones may spoil
The forced produce of your toil?

Have ye leisure, comfort, calm,
Shelter, food, love's gentle balm?
Or what is it ye buy so dear
With your pain and with your fear?

1820

The seed ye sow, another reaps;
The wealth ye find, another keeps;
The robes ye weave, another wears;
The arms ye forge, another bears.

Sow seed—but let no tyrant reap:
Find wealth—let no impostor heap:
Weave robes—let not the idle wear:
Forge arms—in your defence to bear.

Shrink to your cellars, holes, and cells—
In halls ye deck another dwells.
Why shake the chains ye wrought? Ye see
The steel ye tempered glance on ye.

With plough and spade and hoe and loom
Trace your grave and build your tomb,
And weave your winding-sheet—till fair
England be your Sepulchre.

1821

MUTABILITY
William Wordsworth

From low to high doth dissolution climb,
And sink from high to low, along a scale
Of awful notes, whose concord shall not fail;
A musical but melancholy chime,
Which they can hear who meddle not with crime,
Nor avarice, nor over-anxious care.
Truth fails not; but her outward forms that bear
The longest date do melt like frosty rime,
That in the morning whitened hill and plain
And is no more; drop like the tower sublime
Of yesterday, which royally did wear
His crown of weeds, but could not even sustain
Some casual shout that broke the silent air,
Or the unimaginable touch of Time.

1821

THE SKYLARK

James Hogg

    Bird of the wilderness,
    Blithesome and cumberless,
Sweet by thy matin o'er moorland and lea!
    Emblem of happiness,
    Blest is they dwelling-place—
O! to abide in the desert with thee!
    Wild is thy lay and loud,
    Far in the downy cloud,
Love gives it energy, love gave it birth.
    Where, on thy dewy wing,
    Where art thou journeying?
Thy lay is in heaven, thy love in on earth.
    O'er field and fountain sheen,
    O'er moor and mountain green,
O'er the red streamer that heralds the day,
    Over the cloudlet dim,
    Over the rainbow's rim,
Musical cherub, soar, signing, away!
    Then, when the gloaming comes,
    Low in the heather blooms
Sweet will thy welcome and bed of love be!
    Emblem of happiness,
    Blest is thy dwelling-place—
Oh, to abide in the desert with thee!

A BOY'S SONG

James Hogg

Where the pools are bright and deep,
Where the grey trout lies asleep,
Up the river and o'er the lea
That's the way for Billy and me.

Where the blackbird sings the latest,
Where the hawthorn blooms the sweetest,
Where the nestlings chirp and flee,
That's the way for Billy and me.

Where the mowers mow the cleanest,
Where the hay lies thick and greenest,
There to trace the homeward bee,
That's the way for Billy and me.

Where the hazel bank is steepest,
Where the shadow falls the deepest,
Where the clustering nuts fall free,
That's the way for Billy and me.

Why the boys should drive away
Little sweet maidens from the play,
Or love to banter and fight so well,
That's the thing I never could tell.

But this I know, I love to play,
Through the meadow, among the hay;
Up the water and o'er the lea,   1822
That's the way for Billy and me.

1823

ON READING WALTER SCOTT'S "MARMION"
Joanna Baillie

Charm'd by the patriot muse of Flodden Field,
   My country's dearer claims the while forgot,
I almost wish'd that Surry's host might yield,
   And (pardon England) long'd to be a Scot.

For torpid is the heart that doth not feel,
   As he directs, the poet's powerful spell,
When heaven-born genius fires his patriot zeal,
   And bids him sing so sweetly and so well.

And highly too it crown'd my fond desire,
   In this long barren dearth of Southern song,
To hear once more proud Ettrick's living lyre,
   Each glowing chord's harmonious swell prolong;

Whose strains sublime, like deepening thunders, roll
The battle's stormy wave, and fill th' impassioned soul!

1823

ON READING WORDSWORTH'S LINES ON PEELE CASTLE

Mary Shelley

It is with me, as erst with you,
Oh poet, nature's chronicler,
The summer seas have lost their hue
And storm sits brooding everywhere.

The gentlest rustling of the deep
Is but the dirge of him I lost,
And when waves raise their furrows steep,
And bring foam in which is tossed.

A voice I hear upon the wind
Which bids me haste to join him there,
And woo the tempest's breath unkind
Which gives to me a kindred bier.

And when all smooth are ocean's plains
And sails afar are glittering,
The fairest skiff his form contains
To my poor heart's fond picturing.

1825

Then wildly to the beach I rush,
And fain would seize the frailest boat,
And from dull earth the slight hull push,
On dancing waves towards him to float.

"Nor may I e'er again behold
The sea, and be as I have been;
My bitter grief will ne'er grow old,
Nor say I this with mind serene."

For oft I weep in solitude
And shed so many bitter tears,
While on past joys I vainly brood
And shrink in fear from coming years.

WORK WITHOUT HOPE
Samuel Taylor Coleridge

All Nature seems at work. Slugs leave their lair—
The bees are stirring—birds are on the wing—
And Winter slumbering in the open air,
Wears on his smiling face a dream of Spring!
And I the while, the sole unbusy thing,
Nor honey make, nor pair, nor build, nor sing.

   Yet well I ken the banks where amaranths blow,
Have traced the fount whence streams of nectar flow
Bloom, O ye amaranths! bloom for whom ye may,
For me ye bloom not! Glide, rich streams, away!
With lips unbrightened, wreathless brow, I stroll:
And would you learn the spells that drowse my soul?
Work without Hope draws nectar in a sieve,
And Hope without an object cannot live.

TO A SKYLARK
William Wordsworth

1825

Ethereal minstrel! pilgrim of the sky!
Dost thou despise the earth where cares abound?
Or, while the wings aspire, are heart and eye
Both with thy nest upon the dewy ground?
Thy nest which thou canst drop into at will,
Those quivering wings composed, that music still!
Leave to the nightingale her shady wood;
A privacy of glorious light is thine:
Whence thou dost pour upon the world a flood
Of harmony, with instinct more divine:
Type of the wise who soar, but never roam;
True to the kindred points of Heaven and Home!

THE TRUTH OF WOMAN (from *The Betrothed*)
Sir Walter Scott

Woman's faith, and woman's trust—
Write the characters in the dust;
Stamp them on the running stream,
Print them on the moon's pale beam,
And each evanescent letter
Shall be clearer, firmer, better,

And more permanent, I ween,
Than the thing those letters mean.
I have strain'd the spider's thread
'Gainst the promise of a maid;
I have weigh'd a grain of sand
'Gainst her plight of heart and hand;
I told my true love of the token,
How her faith proved light, and her word was broken:
Again her word and truth she plight,
And I believed them again ere night.

THE GRAVES OF A HOUSEHOLD

Felicia Hemans

They grew in beauty, side by side,
    They fill'd one home with glee;—
Their graves are sever'd, far and wide,
    By mount, and stream, and sea.

The same fond mother bent at night
    O'er each fair sleeping brow;
She had each folded flower in sight,—
    Where are those dreamers now?

One, midst the forests of the west,
    By a dark stream is laid—
The Indian knows his place of rest,
    Far in the cedar shade.

1825

The sea, the blue lone sea, hath one,
    He lies where pearls lie deep;
He was the lov'd of all, yet none
    O'er his low bed may weep.

One sleeps where southern vines are drest
    Above the noble slain:
He wrapt his colours round his breast,
    On a blood-red field of Spain.

And one—o'er *her* the myrtle showers
    Its leaves, by soft winds fann'd;
She faded midst Italian flowers,—
    The last of that bright band.

And parted thus they rest, who play'd
    Beneath the same green tree;
Whose voices mingled as they pray'd
    Around one parent knee!

They that with smiles lit up the hall,
    And cheer'd with song the hearth,—
Alas! for love, if *thou* wert all,
    And nought beyond, oh earth!

137

CASABIANCA[15]
Felicia Hemans

The boy stood on the burning deck,
    Whence all but he had fled;
The flame that lit the battle's wreck,
    Shone round him o'er the dead.

Yet beautiful and bright he stood,
    As born to rule the storm;
A creature of heroic blood,
    A proud, though child-like form.

The flames roll'd on—he would not go,
    Without his Father's word;
That father, faint in death below,
    His voice no longer heard.

He call'd aloud—"say, father, say
    If yet my task is done?"
He knew not that the chieftain lay
    Unconscious of his son.

1826

"Speak, Father!" once again he cried,
    "If I may yet be gone!"
—And but the booming shots replied,
    And fast the flames roll'd on.

Upon his brow he felt their breath,
    And in his waving hair;
And look'd from that lone post of death,
    In still, yet brave despair.

And shouted but once more aloud,
    "My father! must I stay?"
While o'er him fast, through sail and shroud,
    The wreathing fires made way.

They wrapt the ship in splendour wild,
    They caught the flag on high,
And stream'd above the gallant child,
    Like banners in the sky.

15 Author's note: "Young Casabianca, a boy about thirteen years old, son to the admiral of the Orient, remained at his post (in the battle of the Nile), after the ship had taken fire, and all the guns had been abandoned, and perished in the explosion of the vessel, when the flames had reached the powder."

There came a burst of thunder sound—
    The boy—oh! where was he?
—Ask of the winds that far around
    With fragments strewed the sea!

With mast, and helm, and pennon fair,
    That well had borne their part—
But the noblest thing which perish'd there
    Was that young faithful heart.

THE HOMES OF ENGLAND
Felicia Hemans

The stately Homes of England,
    How beautiful they stand!
Amidst their tall ancestral trees,
    O'er all the pleasant land!
The deer across their green-sward bound,
    Through shade and sunny gleam;
And the swan glides past them with the sound
    Of some rejoicing stream.

The merry Homes of England!
    Around their hearths by night
What gladsome looks of household love
    Meet in the ruddy light!
There woman's voice flows forth in song,
    Or childhood's tale is told;
Or lips move tunefully along
    Some glorious page of old.

1826

The blessed Homes of England
    How softly on their bowers
Is laid the holy quietness
    That breathes from Sabbath hours!
Solemn, yet sweet, the church-bell's chime
    Floats through their woods at morn;
All other sounds, in that still time,
    Of breeze and leaf are born.

The Cottage Homes of England!
    By thousands, on her plains,
They are smiling o'er the silvery brooks,
    And round the hamlet-fanes.
Through glowing orchards forth they peep,
    Each from its nook of leaves,
And fearless there the lowly sleep,
    As the bird beneath their eaves.

The free, fair Homes of England!
   Long, long, in hut and hall,
May hearts of native proof be rear'd
   To guard each hallow'd wall!
And green for ever be the groves,
   And bright the flowery sod,
Where first the child's glad spirit loves
   Its country and its God!

THE FROZEN SHIP

Letitia Elizabeth Landon

The fair ship cut the billows,
   And her path lay white behind,
And dreamily amid her sails
   Scarce moved the sleeping wind.

The sailors sang their gentlest songs,
   Whose words were home and love;
Waveless the wide sea spread beneath—
   And calm the heaven above.

But as they sung, each voice turn'd low,
   Albeit they knew not why;
For quiet was the waveless sea,
   And cloudless was the sky.

But the clear air was cold as clear;
   'Twas pain to draw the breath;
And the silence and the chill around
   Were e'en like those of death.

Colder and colder grew the air,
   Spell-bound seem'd the waves to be;
And ere night fell, they knew they were lock'd
   In the arms of that icy sea.

Stiff lay the sail, chain-like the ropes,
   And snow pass'd o'er the main;
Each thought, but none spoke, of distant home
   They should never see again.

Each look'd upon his comrade's face,
   Pale as funereal stone;
Yet none could touch the other's hand,
   For none could feel his own.

1826

140

Like statues fix'd , that gallant band
    Stood on the dread deck to die;
The sleet was their shroud, the wind their dirge,
    And their churchyard the sea and the sky.

Fond eyes watch'd by their native shore,
    And prayers to the wild winds gave;
But never again came that stately ship
    To breast the English wave.

Hope grew fear, and fear grew hope,
    Till both alike were done:
And the bride lay down in her grave alone,
    And the mother without her son.

Years pass'd, and of that goodly ship
    Nothing of tidings came;
Till, in after-time, when her fate had grown
    But a tale of fear and a name—

It was beneath a tropic sky
    The tale was told to me;
The sailor who told, in his youth had been
    Over that icy sea.

He said it was fearful to see them stand,
    Nor the living nor yet the dead,
And the light glared strange in the glassy eyes
    Whose human look was fled.

1826

For frost had done one-half life's part,
    And kept them from decay;
Those they loved had moulder'd, but these
    Look'd the dead of yesterday.

Peace to the souls of the graveless dead!
    'Twas an awful doom to dree;
But fearful and wondrous are thy works,
    O God! in the boundless sea!

THE ROYAL LINE
James Henry Leigh Hunt

William I.	The sturdy Conq'ror, politic, severe;
William II.	Light-minded Rufus, dying like the deer;
Henry I.	Beau-clerc, who everything but virtue knew;
Stephen.	Stephen, who graced the lawless sword he drew;
Henry II.	Fine Henry, hapless in his sons and priest;
Richard I.	Richard, the glorious trifler in the East;
John.	John, the mean wretch, tyrant and slave, a liar;
Henry III.	Imbecile Henry, worthy of his sire;
Edward I.	Long-shanks, well nam'd, a great encroacher he;
Edward II.	Edward the minion, dying dreadfully;
Edward III.	The splendid veteran, weak in his decline;
Richard II.	Another minion, sure untimely sign;
Henry IV.	Usurping Lancaster, whom wrongs advance;
Henry V.	Harry the Fifth, the tennis-boy of France;
Henry VI.	The beadsman, praying while his Margaret fought;
Edward IV.	Edward, too sensual for a kindly thought;
Edward V.	The little head, that never wore the crown;
Richard III.	Crookback, to Nature giving frown for frown;
Henry VII.	Close-hearted Henry, the shrewd, carking sire;
Henry VIII.	The British Bluebeard, fat, and full of ire;
Edward VI.	The sickly boy, endowing and endow'd;
Mary.	Ill Mary, lighting many a living shroud;
Elizabeth.	The lion-queen, with her stiff muslin mane;
James I.	The shambling pedant and his minion train;
Charles I.	Weak Charles, the victim of the dawn of right;
Cromwell.	Cromwell, misuser of his home-spun might;
Charles II.	The swarthy scape-grace, all for ease and wit;
James II.	The bigot out of season, forc'd to quit;
William III.	The Dutchman, call'd to see our vessel through;
Anne.	Anna, made great by conquering Marlborough;
George I.	George, vulgar soul, a woman-hated name;
George II.	Another, fonder of his fee than fame;
George III.	A third, too weak, instead of strong, to swerve;
George IV.	And forth, whom *Canning* and Sir Will preserve.

1829

WOMAN AND FAME
Felicia Hemans

Thou hast a charmed cup, O Fame!
   A draught that mantles high,
And seems to lift this earthly frame
   Above mortality.
Away! to me—a woman—bring
Sweet waters from affection's spring.

Thou hast green laurel leaves, that twine
   Into so proud a wreath;
For that resplendent gift of thine,
   Heroes have smiled in death:
Give *me* from some kind hand a flower,
The record of one happy hour!

Thou hast a voice, whose thrilling tone
   Can bid each life-pulse beat
As when a trumpet's note hath blown,
   Calling the brave to meet:
But mine, let mine—a woman's breast,
By words of home-born love be bless'd.

A hollow sound is in thy song,
   A mockery in thine eye,
To the sick heart that doth but long
   For aid, for sympathy—
For kindly looks to cheer it on,
For tender accents that are gone.

Fame, Fame! thou canst not be the stay
   Unto the drooping reed,
The cool fresh fountain in the day
   Of the soul's feverish need:
Where must the lone one turn or flee?—
Not unto thee—oh! not to thee!

1829

1832

THE LITTLE SHROUD[16]
Letitia Elizabeth Landon

She put him on a snow-white shroud,
    A chaplet on his head;
And gather' d early primroses
    To scatter o'er the dead.

She laid him in his little grave—
    'Twas hard to lay him there,
When spring was putting forth its flower,
    And every thing was fair.

She had lost many children—now
    The last of them was gone;
And day and night she sat and wept
    Beside the funeral stone.

One midnight, while her constant tears
    Were falling with the dew,
She heard a voice, and lo! her child
    Stood by her weeping too!

His shroud was damp, his face was white.
    He said,—"I cannot sleep.
Your tears have made my shroud so wet,
    O, mother, do not weep!"

O, love is strong!—the mother's heart
    Was fill'd with tender fears;
o, love is strong!—and for her child
    Her grief restrain'd its tears.

One eve a light shone round her bed,
    And there she saw him stand—
Her infant in his little shroud
    A taper in his hand.

"Lo! mother, see my shroud is dry.
    And I can sleep once more!"
And beautiful the parting smile
    The little infant wore.

And down within the silent grave
    He laid his weary head;
And soon the early violets
    Grew o'er his grassy bed.

The mother went her household ways—
    Again she knelt in prayer,
And only ask'd of Heaven its aid
    Her heavy lot to bear.

---

16 This is a poetic rendition of the story "The Little Shroud" (Das Todtenhemdchen) included in the Grimm Brothers' collection of folk tales, an essential contribution to German Romanticism.

1833

STEAMBOATS, VIADUCTS & RAILWAYS
William Wordsworth

Motions and Means, on land and sea at war
With old poetic feeling, not for this,
Shall ye, by Poets even, be judged amiss!
Nor shall your presence, howsoe'er it mar
The loveliness of Nature, prove a bar
To the Mind's gaining that prophetic sense
Of future change, that point of vision, whence
May be discovered what in soul ye are.
In spite of all that beauty may disown
In your harsh features, Nature doth embrace
Her lawful offspring in Man's art; and Time,
Pleased with your triumphs o'er his brother Space,
Accepts from your bold hands the proffered crown
Of hope, and smiles on you with cheer sublime.

1833

1837

A VOICE FROM THE DUNGEON

Anne Brontë

I'm buried now; I've done with life;
I've done with hate, revenge and strife;
I've done with joy, and hope and love
And all the bustling world above.

Long have I dwelt forgotten here
In pining woe and dull despair;
This place of solitude and gloom
Must be my dungeon and my tomb.

No hope, no pleasure can I find;
I am grown weary of my mind.
Often in balmy sleep I try
To gain a rest from misery.

And in one hour of calm repose
To find a respite from my woes,
But dreamless sleep is not for me
And I am still in misery.

I dream of liberty, 'tis true,
But then I dream of sorrow too,
Of blood and guilt and horrid woes,
Of tortured friends and happy foes;

I dream about the world, but then
I dream of fiends instead of men;
Each smiling hope so quickly fades
And such a lurid gloom pervades

That world—that when I wake and see
Those dreary phantoms fade and flee,
Even in my dungeon I can smile,
And taste of joy a little while.

And yet it is not always so;
I dreamt a little while ago
That all was as it used to be:
A fresh free wind passed over me;

It was a pleasant summer's day,
The sun shone forth with cheering ray,
Methought a little lovely child
Looked up into my face and smiled.

My heart was full, I wept for joy,
It was my own, my darling boy;
I clasped him to my breast and he
Kissed me and laughed in childish glee.

Just then I heard in whisper sweet
A well known voice my name repeat.
His father stood before my eyes;
I gazed at him in mute surprise,

I thought he smiled and spoke to me,
But still in silent ecstasy
I gazed at him; I could not speak;
I uttered one long piercing shriek.

Alas! Alas! That curséd scream
Aroused me from my heavenly dream;
I looked around in wild despair,
I called them, but they were not there;
The father and the child are gone,
And I must live and die alone.

1837

1838

ABOU BEN ADHEM
James Henry Leigh Hunt

Abou Ben Adhem (may his tribe increase!)
Awoke one night from a deep dream of peace,
And saw, within the moonlight in his room,
Making it rich, and like a lily in bloom,
An angel writing in a book of gold:—
Exceeding peace had made Ben Adhem bold,
And to the presence in the room he said,
"What writest thou?"—The vision raised its head,
And with a look made of all sweet accord,
Answered, "The names of those who love the Lord."
"And is mine one?" said Abou. "Nay, not so,"
Replied the angel. Abou spoke more low,
But cheerly still; and said, "I pray thee, then,
Write me as one that loves his fellow-men."

1838

The angel wrote, and vanished. The next night
It came again, with a great wakening light,
And showed the names whom love of God had blessed,
And lo! Ben Adhem's name led all the rest.

1846

NO COWARD SOUL IS MINE
Emily Brontë

No coward soul is mine
No trembler in the world's storm-troubled sphere
I see Heaven's glories shine
And Faith shines equal arming me from Fear.

O God within my breast
Almighty ever-present Deity
Life, that in me hast rest,
As I Undying Life, have power in Thee!

Vain are the thousand creeds
That move men's hearts, unutterably vain,
Worthless as withered weeds
Or idlest froth amid the boundless main,

To waken doubt in one
Holding so fast by thy infinity,
So surely anchored on
The steadfast rock of Immortality.

With wide-embracing love
Thy spirit animates eternal years
Pervades and broods above,
Changes, sustains, dissolves, creates and rears

Though earth and moon were gone
And suns and universes ceased to be
And Thou wert left alone
Every Existence would exist in Thee.

There is not room for Death
Nor atom that his might could render void
Since thou art Being and Breath
And what thou art may never be destroyed.

1846

Year	Publications	Events
1786	Robert Burns, *Poems Chiefly in the Scottish Dialect*	
1789	William Blake, *Songs of Innocence*	George III recovers French Revolution begins with the storming of the Bastille George Washington inaugurated as 1st president of the United States. Fletcher Christian leads the Mutiny on the *Bounty*.
1790	Edmund Burke, *Reflections on the Revolution in France* Mary Wollstonecraft, *Vindication of the Rights of Men*	
1791	Paine, *The Rights of Man*	Louis XVI and his family caught fleeing the country Passing of French constitution Rebellion in Haiti under Toussaint L'Ouverture
1792	Mary Wollstonecraft, *Vindication of the Rights of Women*	French royals imprisoned; nobles slaughtered by masses in France; Louis XVI goes on trial for treason; 1st French republic Percy Shelley born
1793	Godwin, *Political Justice*	Louis XVI sentenced to death; reign of terror begins; Marie Antoinette executed France declares war on England and Netherlands
1794	Blake, *Songs of Innocence and Experience*	French National Convention proclaims slavery abolished Coup of Thermidor: fall of Robespierre in Paris

Year	Publications	Events
1795		John Keats born
1796	Chatterton, *Poetical Works* (posthumous)	Robert Burns dies Threat of French invasion William Godwin and Mary Wollstonecraft marry Mary Wollstonecraft Godwin (future Mary Shelley) born Mary Wollstonecraft dies
1797	Robert Southey, *Poems*; *Letters written in Spain and Portugal*	
1798	Coleridge and Wordsworth, *Lyrical Ballads* Coleridge, "Frost at Midnight," "France, an Ode"	Nelson destroys French fleet in the battle of the Nile
1799	Burns, *Works* (posthumous)	Napoleon becomes first Consul after a coup
1800	Wordsworth and Coleridge, *Lyrical Ballads* (2 vols., Preface, 1798 poems and new poems)	Act of Union with Ireland
1801	Southey, *Thalaba the Destroyer*	
1802	Joanna Baillie, *Plays on the Passions* (2nd vol., signed with her name) Walter Scott, *Minstrelsy of the Scottish Border*	Peace of Amiens halts hostilities between England and France Napoleon made life consul
1803		War with France declared
1804	William Blake, *Milton*	Napoleon crowned emperor
1806	Walter Scott, *Ballads and Lyrical Pieces*	
1807	Wordsworth, *Poems in Two Volumes* Byron, *Hours of Idleness*	Slave trade abolished

152

Year	Publications	Events
1808	Walter Scott, *Marmion*	Peninsular War begins
1809	Byron, *English Bards and Scotch Reviewers*	Thomas Paine dies
1810	Scott, *The Lady of the Lake* Percy Shelley, *Original Poetry by Victor and Cazire*	
1811	Austen, *Sense and Sensibility*	Prince of Wales becomes Prince regent Luddite insurgency Shelley expelled from Oxford for publication of "The Necessity of Atheism"
1812	Byron, *Childe Harold's Pilgrimage* (Cantos I and II)	Britain at war with America Napoleon invades Russia then retreats with heavy losses
1813	Austen, *Pride and Prejudice* Shelley, *Queen Mab*	Southey becomes Poet laureate Leigh Hunt imprisoned (until 1815) for libelling the Prince Regent
1814	Byron, *The Corsair* Leigh Hunt, *Feast of the Poets* (revised edition)	Napoleon abdicates and is exiled to Elba Peace between Britain and the United States
1815		Byron marries Battle of Waterloo; Napoleon surrenders and is later exiled on the Isle of St. Helena
1816	Coleridge, *Christabel and Other Poems*	Shelley marries Mary Godwin Leigh Hunt's essay on Shelley and Keats in *The Examiner*
1817	Byron, *Manfred* Coleridge, *Biographia Literaria* Keats, *Poems*	Jane Austen dies Attack on Keats in the *Quarterly Review*

Year	Publications	Events
1818	Hazlitt, *Lectures on the English Poets* Keats, *Endymion* Mary Shelley, *Frankenstein*	Shelley leaves England for the last time
1819	Shelley, *Mask of Anarchy* Byron, *Don Juan*	Peterloo massacre
1820	Blake finishes *Jerusalem* Keats, *Lamia; Eve of St. Agnes* Shelley, *Prometheus Unbound*	George III dies Ascension of George IV
1821	Byron, *Cain* Shelley, *Adonais; A Defense of Poetry*	Keats dies Famine in Ireland Napoleon dies Greek War of Independence begins
1822	Wordsworth, *Ecclesiastical Sketches*	Shelley dies
1824	Byron, *The Deformed Transformed*	Byron dies
1825	Coleridge, *Aids to Reflection*	Anna Laetitia Barbauld dies Stockton and Darlington railways opened
1827		Blake dies
1830		King George IV dies and is succeeded by William IV
1832		Great Reform Act extends suffrage to 1 in 5 men Walter Scott dies
1834	Worsdworth, "Sonnets" (*Poetical Works*)	Slavery abolished in British Empire Coleridge dies Charles Lamb dies
1843		Southey dies and Wordsworth replaces him as Poet laureate

Year	Publications	Events
1846	Publication of Poems by Currer, Acton and Ellis Bell (the Brontë sisters)	
1847	Publication of *Jane Eyre, Wuthering Heights,* and *Agnes Grey*	
1848		Emily Brontë dies
1849		Anne Brontë dies
1850	Wordsworth, *The Prelude*	Wordsworth dies

INDEX OF AUTHORS AND TITLES

CPSIA information can be obtained
at www.ICGtesting.com
Printed in the USA
LVHW08s0300260718
584965LV00003B/22/P